CHRISTIAN HOPE

CHRISTIAN HOPE

by
JOHN MACQUARRIE

*Lady Margaret Professor of Divinity,
University of Oxford, and Canon of
Christ Church*

MOWBRAYS
LONDON & OXFORD

© John Macquarrie 1978

ISBN 0 264 66064 1

First published by A. R. Mowbray & Co Ltd
Saint Thomas House, Becket Street
Oxford, OX1 1SJ

Filmset in 'Monophoto' Baskerville 10 on 11 pt. by
Richard Clay (The Chaucer Press), Ltd., Bungay, Suffolk
and printed in Great Britain by
Fletcher & Son Ltd., Norwich

In Memoriam
Cyril Richardson
1906–1976

Contents

'Christianity ... seems like a final emergence of what religion is—a *total hope*, and an explosive one.'

Ernst Bloch.

Preface

Hope is one of the great themes of Christian faith, but hope is also as wide as humanity itself. This book tries to reach a clearer understanding of what hope is, and what hope we ourselves can entertain. Beginning from the universal presence of hope in mankind, it sets out the specifically Christian hope, from its sources in the Bible through its development in Christian theology to its significance in the contemporary world.

Christ Church,   *John Macquarrie*
Oxford,
Eastertide, 1978.

I
What Is Hope?

It seems safe to say that the expression, 'Christian hope,' is likely to conjure up in the minds of most people who hear it pictures of heaven and of a blissful life to come. In the popular understanding— or misunderstanding—of it, Christian hope has come to be visualized almost entirely in other-worldly terms. Thus, to the sceptic, Christian hope looks like an escape mechanism or a comforting illusion. It is cynically described as 'pie in the sky' and seen as a tranquillizer which diverts attention and energy from the problems of our actual existence and so lessens the hope that these problems might be over-come. The classic criticism of an escapist hope was voiced by Karl Marx: 'Religion is the sigh of the oppressed creature, the opium of the people. The abolition of religion as the illusory happiness of the people is required for their real happiness. The demand to give up the illusions about its condition is the demand to give up a condition which needs illusions. The criticism of religion disillusions man, to make him think and act and shape his reality like a man who has been disillusioned and has come to reason, so that he will revolve round himself and therefore round his true sun. Religion is only the illusory sun which revolves round man as long as he does not revolve round himself.'[1]

Of course, one can say that Marx has grossly caricatured and distorted Christian hope. Yet the caricature is only possible because Christians themselves (and not just at the level of popular religion) have been one-sided in their way of thinking about Christian hope. It is because they have made it such an other-worldly affair that the Marxist critique of heaven has been so persuasive. So right at the beginning of this study of Christian hope, I wish to dissociate it firmly from that distorted form of Christian hope which loses sight of this world and our life in the world in order, ostrich-like, to become immersed in a beyond. Christian hope is a total hope, and it touches on all aspects of human life, both individual and social. As a total hope, it is a hope not limited or nullified by death. Indeed, I would have no hesitation in calling it a 'supernatural' hope, in the sense that it looks for possibilities beyond those which we know in our everyday 'natural' existence. But a truly total hope is a hope so large and many-sided that we impoverish and misrepresent it if we lay all the stress on its supernatural and other-worldly aspects. It is in the first instance a hope arising in the history of this world and having relevance for our life in this world.

Thus, before anything is said about the specifically Christian hope, we shall try to grasp the nature of hope as a universal human phenomenon, one which appears in many forms and has many objects, from the most trivial to the most profound. Then, when we are in a position to go on to reflect on Christian hope, we shall be conscious of how it is related to all the other hopes of the human race, and we shall be less likely to fall into that widespread error of separating it off as a highly peculiar kind of hope, having little or nothing to do with the hopes that belong to our everyday life in the world.

Admittedly, there are some theologians who would question the procedure that has been proposed here. They would say that Christian hope is in fact so peculiar, so distinct and unique, that it cannot be understood as a special case of some general phenomenon of hope. They would say that our only chance of properly under-standing this Christian hope is to be prepared to confront it in all its particularity and concreteness, in its connection with specific historical events which Christians claim to have been actions of God; and they might even urge that only after one has understood some-thing of the distinctively Christian hope, which is hope at its deepest and fullest, can one usefully begin to reflect on the universal phenomenon of hope.

Let me at once concede that there is some cogency to such arguments. Christian hope is inextricably tied up with the biblical tradition, and can be properly understood only in the setting of the quite specific beliefs and historical happenings in which it originated. Furthermore, there are new dimensions in Christian hope that cannot be derived from consideration of the general human experience of hope. These are points which we must not forget, or we shall be in danger of presenting a defective and impoverished interpretation of Christian hope, one in which it has been deprived of its distinctive power and made to conform to preconceived patterns drawn from general experience. Our own age is perhaps especially guilty of a tendency to level down everything that is exceptional and original to the level of the universally intelligible and acceptable. But if Christianity—or any other religion—brings revelation in the sense of disclosing the new and letting us become aware of what had previously been hidden from us, then we must be careful to let it speak for itself and not force it into moulds that we have already set up on the basis of earlier and perhaps less adequate experience. We must heed some salutary words of Karl Barth: 'When the Word of God meets us, we are laden with the images, ideas and certainties which we ourselves have formed about God, the world and ourselves. In the fog of this intellectual life of ours the Word of God, which is clear in itself, always becomes obscure. It can become clear to us only when this fog breaks and dissolves.'[2] Possibly these words apply nowhere more forcibly than they do in this area of Christian hope. Christ has opened a new hope for the human race, and if we refuse to let that hope confront us in its own integrity, trying instead to assimilate it to a prior understanding of what all hope must be, then we may very well find it confused, alien and unacceptable—not because it is confused, alien and unacceptable, but because we have already decided what the scope and limits of hope are.

So much has to be conceded, and not only conceded but asserted, and continually borne in mind. Nevertheless, in spite of the danger, we adhere to the proposal that we begin with a general phenomenological description of hope. The reason is that if Christian hope is not related at the outset to the perspective of human hope in general, then we run that greater danger of falling into the all too common misunderstanding of Christian hope as something quite otherworldly in character and thus unrelated to the ordinary hopes of the mass of mankind.

But it should be clearly understood that in making this methodological choice, we are not choosing one way to the complete rejection of the other. There is no absolute disjunction between the two. As in all interpretation, there cannot fail to be a measure of reciprocity. We can come to an understanding of the Christian hope only because we already have from common experience some understanding of what hope is—and the more this understanding has been clarified, the better; yet we must also expect that if Christian hope has the unique depth and totality claimed for it, and is therefore truly revelatory, then in the light of it we shall be led to a new understanding of the hope that we have come to know in general experience.

1. *Structures of Hope*

We begin then with hope in its simplest and most widespread form. We have already used the expression 'universal phenomenon' in connection with hope, and it does seem that it is coextensive with human life itself. Wherever people work to produce something, wherever they cultivate the fields, wherever they marry, wherever they found and raise families, wherever they learn or teach, wherever they engage in political activities, there is hope. For in all these activities and in a host of others that have not been mentioned, there is an affirmation of the future, a trust in the future, an investment in the future. It seems that in almost everything we do, we are projecting ourselves ahead of ourselves, and we are doing so in the expectation or at least in the faith that some goal will be achieved. If as Feuerbach claimed, 'hope is only faith in relation to the future,'[3] then virtually everything that we do is done hopefully.

This low-keyed hopefulness that seems to pervade almost all human activities I have described as hope in 'its simplest and most widespread form.' Perhaps it would be more accurate to say that it is hope in a diffuse, implicit form. It is hope that has not yet been explicitly formulated in words. It is a pre-reflective hope which however may and does rise to the level of a conscious hope from time to time and in one activity or another. Perhaps this pre-reflective hope should not properly be called hope, but is rather the basis or condition of hope already there in the constitution of human existence as the fundamental tendency of the human being toward hoping. But whatever we may call it or however we may describe it, this root of hoping is an undeniable fact in human nature as we know it in ourselves or observe it in others.

A few philosophers have indeed directed attention to this phenomenon of diffused hopefulness in all human action. Gabriel Marcel, for instance, talks of an ' "I hope" of a very low order,' or of hope in its 'diluted' form, and seeks to pass from that to the understanding of the same experience 'at its point of complete saturation.'[4] The suggestion is that even the most sophisticated human hopes do not appear suddenly out of the blue, but are developments out of that tacit hopefulness which seems to be diffused through all human existing and acting.

But although hope—or, at least, a tendency to hope—is apparently very widespread in human life, it is not easy to define or describe it. Is it simply a passion or emotion, the opposite emotion to fear? Is it a biological mechanism, the function of which is to spur the human race on? Is it, as many Christian moral theologians have held, a theological virtue, to be ranked with faith and love? Or is it a veiled belief about the world and man's place in it—perhaps a comforting illusory belief, generated by wishful thinking?

There would seem to be elements of truth in all these ways of talking about hope. Its character is complex and inclusive. Hope has emotional, volitional and intellectual aspects, and it can be either well or ill founded. I propose to call hope an 'attitude.' By this I mean that it is a set or disposition of the whole person, a stance or posture which one takes up toward experience or sectors of experience, and from which one relates to such experience.

Attitudes are not to be dismissed as non-cognitive, for the attitudes of mature persons are in part based on what they take to be well founded beliefs about the world and society. The attitudes of such persons are never adopted uncritically. On the other hand, attitudes are not simply beliefs. They include some definite 'feel' for the world, and thus give some definite colour or tone to experience. Such attitudes also promote some kinds of behaviour rather than others, and encourage a measure of consistency in behaviour. Hope, we may say, is a fundamental human attitude in which it is possible to discern many facets.

Let us consider first the emotional facet. Hope is an emotion, but not a mere emotion—though, indeed, one would have to question what is meant by the expression 'mere emotion' in any case. Unless one held to the old-fashioned idea of a 'faculty psychology,' that is to say, one in which the mind was supposed to have separate faculties roughly analogous to the several organs of the body, so that one could assign thinking to one faculty, feeling to another, and so on, then one would have to recognize that the distinction we make between thinking, feeling and willing occurs only within a totality of which these activities are inseparable aspects. That totality is a complete state of mind, or rather a complete state of body-mind. As an attitude, hope has this kind of inclusiveness. One may distinguish within it an emotional aspect, but this is always the accompaniment of thinking and willing, and cannot stand apart from them.

All our thinking and acting take place against a background of changing emotional moods, such as joy, boredom, sorrow, anxiety and many others. These are indexes or registers of the way in which we are at any time relating to our environment—not only the physical environment, but the people whom we are meeting in it. Hope is one of the brighter and more positive moods. It includes elements of trust and expectancy, and therefore the hopeful person tends to be outgoing and open toward his environment. He relates to it (including the people in it) in a mainly affirmative way.

This can be seen more clearly if we consider that emotion which is usually held to be the opposite of hope, namely, fear. We could describe fear as a sombre mood and a negative index of the environment. The fearing person feels himself threatened by persons, things or events in the environment, and so he is on the defensive. He is distrustful of the environment, and thus he is unwilling to commit himself to it and tends to withdraw into himself.

Of course, in practice, hope and fear alternate, and sometimes other moods supervene. Most opposing moods and attitudes show a kind of ambivalence. Each tends to pass into its opposite, and perhaps neither could be found apart from the foil provided by its opposite. Faith and doubt offer a good illustration. Can there be a genuine faith that has never experienced doubt, or can there be found doubt that does not presuppose and even seek the possibility of faith?

Hope is always vulnerable, and it may quickly turn to fear. Obviously, too, it is sometimes prudent to fear, and a bland hope that had never known fear would be perhaps as inauthentic as a faith that had never known doubt. Yet while hope and fear go together in human experience, one or other may predominate. There are hopeful natures and fearful natures, by which I mean that some people tend on the whole to live in a hopeful mood, others in a fearful one. Even entire generations may, in different periods of history or in different cultural situations, display either a hopeful or a fearing relation to the environment. For instance, the early generations of settlers in the United States were characterized by a pioneering and often utopian spirit. The hopeful mood encourages outgoingness, willingness for experiment and change, even adventure. In such a mood, the environment seems fluid and able to be moulded. On the other hand, the fearing mood clings to the familiar, eschewing innovation or any kind of relation that would make the people concerned more open to the hostile forces which they believe to be threatening them.

One apparent difference which may call in question the contrast we have developed between hope and fear is that in the case of fear (as with many other emotions) it is possible to give a fairly specific description of certain physical (bodily) states which accompany the emotion or help to constitute it, whereas it does not seem possible to give such a description in the case of hope. When a person is in a state of fear, his heart beats faster, there are changes in the circulation of the blood, the suprarenal capsules pour out adrenalin, and so on. But are there any bodily symptoms of hope? Certainly, one cannot specify them with the same precision. But I do not think this means that hope has no emotional side to it, or that it is a purely 'spiritual' emotion. Hope, like all emotion, has its bodily as well as its mental expression, or, better expressed, it is psychosomatic. Hope surely braces the nerves and heightens vitality. If we find it difficult to specify the bodily meaning of hope, this is perhaps because hope tends to be a fairly settled disposition, whereas fear is an emotion that may suddenly arise and just as suddenly subside. This point may be verified if we think for a moment of disappointment, the mood which arises when a hope is dashed. When someone has undergone an acute disappointment, he may very well say that he has been 'deflated.' The bracing expectancy of hope has been suddenly relaxed, vitality and energy seem to have flowed away, and the disappointed person quite literally wilts. 'Hope deferred makes the heart sick' (Prov. 13, 12). This should not surprise us, for if hope has been truly defined as an attitude and so as belonging to the whole person, then it must have its bodily aspects, for a person is not mere spirit but a psychosomatic entity.

From this discussion of hope in its emotional aspect, we turn to the closely related topic of the volitional aspect of hope. We have noted that in traditional Christian moral theology, hope has been reckoned along with faith and love as one of the theological virtues. What sense does it make to talk of hope as a virtue? How can we ascribe to hope a volitional aspect, or see it as leading to a certain kind of action? Such ways of talking about hope have their sense within the context of Aristotelian and Thomistic ethics. These are theories of ethics which stress virtue, character, habit, as distinguished from those theories (such as Kantian ethics) which stress moral acts and their conformity to rules of conduct. Admittedly, a character or a virtue is built up through habitually acting in a certain way, and even the emotions can be trained so as to become incorporated into character. But a character once formed becomes itself a source of actions, for it then moves us to act in some ways rather than in others. It is in some such way that we can think of the formation of a hopeful character and understand how hope may be conceived as a virtue built into such a character. So understood, hope is a formed disposition of the will. By this is meant that hope helps to unify our actions into consistent policies, directed toward goals consonant with the character of the agent. It is through the virtue of hope that a person directs his actions to goals that lie ahead, sometimes quite far ahead, and pledges his future in their pursuit. Here we have in mind something more explicit than just that general inarticulate hopefulness which, as we have seen, can be said to be present in almost any human activity. Hope can only begin to have its definite influence on action and to produce policies of action when it has been made more specific and raised to the level of a settled disposition.

I would like to make three points which will fill out in more detail the volitional role of hope. They concern: hope in relation to freedom; hope as moral dynamic; and hope as moral and social critique.

The relation of hope to *freedom* was already hinted at when we noted that the emotional mood of hope relates us to the environment as to something having fluidity and not yet rigidly determined in its shape. Such an environment is open to the possibility of change through human action. In a world where the course of events was already fully determined in advance, there would be no place for hope—at least, not for anything more than a pale minimal kind of hope, the mere ghost of hope in its fulness. That is to say, there could be the wishful longing that things might get better in one respect or another, but this could scarcely be more than a passive waiting. It could not be an active hope, dedicating the will and energies to chosen goals. Hope implies that there is, so to speak, an empty space before us that affords us room for action; or, to put it in a slightly different way, an open road along which we can choose to move. Where everything is foreclosed, there is no hope. Thus hope is inseparable from human freedom and human transcendence. This in turn means that hope belongs essentially to any truly personal existence. Where freedom is denied, whether in practical terms through oppression or in theoretical terms through some deterministic ideology, hope is denied also; and where hope is denied, persons are being destroyed, for to be a person means, among other things, to be constantly projecting oneself in hope toward goals in which personal being will find fuller expression and satisfaction. So we can say that where there is hope, there is freedom; and where there is freedom, there is hope.

We touch next on hope as the *dynamic of action*. People act only if they hope to attain the goal of their actions. If the world is, as some writers have believed, absurd and pointless, so that man's best efforts are doomed to frustration, then it is hard to see that there would be any incentive to choose one course of action rather than another. In particular, it is hard to see how people could make moral choices involving great effort and even sacrifice. Such choices are only made because there is faith in the future, that is to say, hope. To be sure, such hope is compatible with the acknowledgement that much moral striving does seem to come to nothing and that sometimes the noblest human hopes are shattered. But (as we shall see in more detail later) hope is not optimism, nor does hope carry the demand that every worthy design of action must be realized. Indeed, there are forms of optimism and of the belief in 'progress' that are just as inimical to genuine hope as the belief (if anyone indeed holds it) that in the long run nothing really matters. Both extreme pessimism and extreme optimism may very well lead to a deadening of the will, for what is the point of putting any energy into one's actions if one is already persuaded that things will turn out one way or the other in any case? Hope has a humility and a tentativeness that puts it in a different category. Such hope does not count on success or succumb to the illusion of progress, but it does inspire action because of the faith that success and advance are possible in this world, whatever the obstacles in the way. St. Thomas put it very well when he wrote: 'Hope's object is a good that lies in the future and that is difficult but possible to attain.'[5] This is the kind of hope that is the true dynamic of human striving and makes possible the patient but tenacious pursuit of the good.

I have said that hope also contributes to the life of action a *moral and social critique*, and this is a point that should not be forgotten. Hope creates discontent. The vision of a future good makes us dissatisfied with current evils. Of course, these remarks have to be interpreted with some care. Not all discontent is good, and not all of it flows from hope. In a time of expanding affluence, we often hear the expression 'rising expectations' and sometimes this expression is simply a euphemism for concupiscence, the inordinate desire to possess more and more. So far as this results from the exaltation of having above being, it proceeds from the spirit of acquisitiveness, not from that of hope. That kind of discontent is likely in the long run to be destructive. But the discontent arising from hope is creative. It comes from visions of the future—not utopian visions, but, to quote again St. Thomas' words, visions of 'a good that lies in the future and that is difficult but possible to attain.' In the case of the individual, it may be an understanding of himself as he might be, and one which condemns his present condition. On a larger scale, there may be visions of peace and justice that make us dissatisfied with the world as we know it today. Such hopes serve as a critique of the present, provide a dynamic for action toward the future, and awaken us to the reality of our freedom and transcendence.

Once again, what I have been saying may be made clearer if we consider briefly the opposite case. The opposite of the virtue of hope is the vice of despair. In despair, a person surrenders the possibility of action, for all courses of action seem equally futile. His mind is prey to apathy and indifference, and the result is inaction. (It has often been noted that what we call 'desperate' acts of rebellion or even self-destruction come not at the depth of despair but after that point has been passed and expectations are beginning to rise and some action becomes possible again.) Needless to say, there is a broad spectrum of possible attitudes between hope and despair, and there may be inaction which does not have anything to do with the paralysis of despair. Prudence may sometimes counsel resignation in the face of intractable circumstances, but this would not be the inaction of despair or the dissolution of hope into despair. If hope is aimed at that which is 'difficult but not impossible,' then inaction and resignation will sometimes be based on a judgment about what is or is not possible in a given situation. There are circumstances in which resignation does not necessarily mean the abandonment of a fundamental hopefulness. Resignation need not be passive surrender; it may be an active acceptance of the intractable circumstances of the situation, followed by a new attempt to face and deal with the situation including these threatening circumstances. In this connection, it is useful to recall the prayer associated with the great Christian realist, Reinhold Niebuhr: 'God, give us grace to accept with serenity the things that cannot be changed, courage to change the things that should be changed, and the wisdom to distinguish the one from the other.'[6] The use of the word 'serenity' in this prayer is very significant. Serenity is equanimity, an affirmative composed accepting frame of mind, and one that testifies to the inward strength of the serene person. It is completely different from the apathy of despair, for that is an emptiness and powerlessness, revealing that the person who has fallen victim to such apathy has been drained of his resources. Thus, although hope normally spurs and sustains action, it knows also how to be quiet and patient.

Our discussion of hope up to this point has shown us how, considered in its emotional aspect, hope consists in an outgoing and trusting mood toward the environment, while, in its volitional aspect, it promotes affirmative courses of action. But hope has also its cognitive or intellectual aspect, and this may be finally what is of most interest. Hope is not just feeling or striving; it carries in itself a definite way of understanding both ourselves and the environing process within which human life has its setting. Particular beliefs about ourselves and the world underlie and express themselves in all experiences of hope. At the emotional and volitional levels, these beliefs may not yet have been articulated, but they are already latent, and we have now to think out what these cognitive elements in the experience of hope are. When we begin to explore all the implications of hope, we find that the underlying beliefs are both extensive and important.

We may conveniently begin with the vocabulary of hope, for the very language that we use in the discussion of hope sketches out a way of conceiving man's place in the world. We talk of change, possibility, transformation, the new, the better—even of salvation and revolution and utopia! This vocabulary (or, if you prefer, the categories or concepts expressed in the vocabulary) makes sense only in a world that is, so to speak, on the move and that has some openness of texture. For instance, hope implies the possibility of change, but not just any or every change. The concept of change, as seen from the viewpoint of hope, is quite a subtle one. In the first place, such change demands some continuity. In change, that which is at present the case is not merely replaced but is actually transformed, so that there is both identity and difference. Furthermore, the change which is of interest to hope is change that brings the new. That is to say, it is not just a reshuffling of patterns, but the creation of genuine novelty. Again, hope is not interested in change for change's sake, but in change for the better, where the better is understood in terms of the deepening and enhancing of personal and communal life. This very concept of change, implicit in hope itself, posits a world in which, as we have said, there is some openness of texture. Here we are reminded of our earlier discussion of the role of hope in action, for we have seen that such hope-inspired action would be impossible in a world where all events were rigidly determined in advance. In that case, not hopeful action but submissive resignation would be the proper attitude of man. Even the 'metaphysical rebellion' advocated by Camus would scarcely be possible. He calls it man's 'protest against his condition and against the whole of creation' and also 'a prolonged protest against death,' and he knows that these limits to human existence are not going to be changed by protest. But the very protest has value and constitutes a tiny area of openness amid the general absurdity.[7]

To use the vocabulary of hope and to accept its categories entails a very different kind of world from that of the determinist. The world seen from the viewpoint of hope, *sub specie spei*, as we might say, is one in which, first of all, human beings themselves have some freedom. They can initiate events on the basis of the goals that they have set themselves and they are capable of self-transcendence, both in their individual and social existence. Furthermore, it is a world in which even the non-human reality must have some degree of plasticity and fluidity, for it is conceived as an unfinished world, still in process of creation, so that it can be moulded one way or another and can become, from a human point of view, a better environment, first more tolerable and then more fulfilling. The world is in fact seen as a project of man's existence and transcendence. Admittedly, the world already has a givenness, as does the human existent himself. But the world is not just a given reality, still less a ready-made one, but has always a certain futural quality about it. We are coming to be in a world that is coming to be, everything has not been decided and laid down in advance. Thus there is some scope for shaping the future, and this is what makes hope possible. We can say then that some such conception of worldhood and reality is a postulate of hope.

The presuppositions of hope can be teased out further. We have already noted that if the world were utterly evil or absurd, hope would be impossible and one could only despair. But now it is equally important to note on the other hand that if this were the best of all possible worlds, hope would be superfluous and we could only accept the world as it is, with whatever gratitude or resentment each of us might feel able to bring to that acceptance. So we must affirm that hope is possible only in an ambiguous world, a world in which all is not utterly bad and yet one in which nothing is perfect either. This would, of course, be the case in an unfinished world where creation is still going on and in which man is summoned to play a responsible part in the creative process.

What has just been said allows me to come back to a question which was briefly mentioned at an earlier stage—the question of the distinction between hope and optimism. This distinction, I believe, is a sharp one, and so important that it needs to be stressed, for hope can only suffer when it is confused with that counterfeit, optimism. Both hope and optimism stand opposed to pessimism, but they also differ radically from each other. Optimism, whether it is an illicit generalization from theories of evolution or whether it depends on a humanistic doctrine of progress or whether it is derived from a simplistic religious belief that God orders everything for the best, is a philosophy that misses the ambiguity of the world and fails to consider seriously its evil and negative features. Thus, in practice, optimism is frequently brash, arrogant, complacent and insensitive. Ronald Gregor Smith wrote feelingly on the subject: 'The countless individuals who have suffered, the great anonymous host of sufferers of torments at the hands of men, of injustice, of misery, of meaninglessness, of pain of body and agony of spirit, are a cloud of witnesses who point the finger of scorn upon all the neat and tidy optimisms which try to sweep all this accumulation of suffering under the carpet and offer us a tidy scheme.'[8] The reader will remember that the adjectives we have applied to hope are very different—we have called it 'humble,' 'vulnerable,' 'tentative' and we might have added 'sensitive' and 'compassionate.' In contrast to all the optimisms that proclaim themselves, true hope lives in the awareness of the world's evils, sufferings and lacks. Hope must remain vulnerable to evidences that count against it, humble in the face of the evils that have to be transformed, and, above all, compassionate toward those whose experience has been such that their hopes have grown dim or have even been dissolved in despair.

Two points that have arisen in this discussion of the cognitive aspects of hope call for further examination. One is the creative role of hope, as cooperating in the shaping of an unfinished world. The other comes from the recognition of the ambiguity of the world and the warning against optimism, and has to do with the criticism of what may be called the pathology of hope.

Beginning with the creativity of hope, we note that the intellectual activity by which man exercises his creativity is the imagination. Hope is imaginative. It can visualize a state of affairs not yet existing, and, more than that, it can visualize the new. Admittedly, the imagination can work only on the raw material supplied by experience, yet its work is not just that of reshuffling and rearranging the given. The imagination can reach to the vision of that which is new and unprecedented. For instance, one could say that the founding fathers of the United States certainly drew on experience when they framed a constitution for the emerging nation, but one could also claim that the nation so born was a new political phenomenon and to that extent a product of creative vision. I have deliberately chosen this example from the political sphere, because we usually think of imagination in relation to literature and the arts, and forget that it has a much wider significance, not only in science but over the whole area of planning, which seems to have become a necessary feature of life in our mass societies. Planning (if it is to be anything more than the tiresome manipulation of people) needs both hope and the imagination of hope. As Moltmann has remarked, 'Unless hope has been aroused and is alive, there can be no stimulation for planning;' though we must note that he adds almost immediately, 'Without planning there can be no realistic hope.'[9] Hope then needs imaginative thought, and planning for the future of mankind, if it is to be anything more than bureaucratic calculation or doctrinaire politics, needs hope with all its dynamic and openness. The kind of planning which people rightly resent is that which rigidly lays down the course of future development. An approach to the future that is truly hopeful and creative allows room for new developments not foreseen by those who first entertained the hope. Again, the example of the United States is of interest at this point. Two hundred years after the birth of that country, it both fulfils and yet does not fulfil what its founders visualized for it. In some ways it has fulfilled what they hoped for it; in other ways it has failed to fulfil the hope; and in yet other ways, it has more than fulfilled the hopes, in the sense that it has gone on to develop new implications of the constitution, implications which were not explicitly present to the minds of the founders, yet which may certainly claim to be consonant with their intentions. This question of how a hope is fulfilled has quite considerable significance for the intellectual aspects of hope, for it raises the further question of how a hope is falsified. This is a question we shall have to consider in detail later,[10] but for the present it is important to note that if we recognize the role of creative imagination in hope, then we must also recognize that it is impossible to say in advance precisely how a hope is going to be fulfilled, for the very nature of hope permits or even encourages new and unsuspected developments in its unfolding.

The second point we were to examine concerned the criticism of the pathology of hope. The second half of our quotation from Moltmann becomes relevant here: 'Without planning there can be no realistic hope.' Imaginative hope can run riot and it often does so. One has only to recall the wilder fantasies of apocalyptic or the delusions of utopia to see how hope can become diseased and can mislead people, even seducing them from their true obligations. Thus to the intellectual or cognitive element in hope belongs the task of criticism. We must notice that this is a different kind of criticism from the kind which we mentioned in discussing hope in relation to will. There we saw that a hopeful vision of a future state of affairs can act as a moral or political critique of the existing state of affairs, making us dissatisfied with it. But here we are concerned with the reciprocal but equally necessary critique of hope's object by referring it to the hard facts of the empirical situation. Some words of Rubem Alves are worth quoting: 'Visions of the future not extracted from history or which do not take the movement of freedom as their basis, cannot be called hope; they are forms of alienation, illusions which cannot inform history because of their unrelatedness to the way of operation of freedom in the world.'[11] Hope can remain healthy and be prevented from lapsing into optimism and other aberrations only so long as its intellectual side continues to criticize the objects which hope proposes. No doubt there will sometimes be tension between the imaginative and the critical exercise of thought in relation to hope, but this is a tension known in other areas as well.

2. *Total Hope and Religion*

These reflections on the intellectual implicates of the attitude of hope lead us to the question of whether, if pressed far enough, they bring us to some religious belief. Does hope imply religion as its ultimate underpinning? Let it be said at once that there is no clear or easy answer to this question. In recent years, some theologians have been rather free in bandying about the words, 'Where there is hope, there is religion'—words derived from the philosopher Ernst Bloch, but often quoted without sufficient attention to his own explication of them.[12] But while we must be on our guard against attempts to make the connection between hope and faith in too facile a manner, the affinities between the two call for an investigation. Are hope and faith finally separable? James Alfred Martin has remarked: 'Analysts of the language of faith who overlook or ignore the role of hope have an inadequate understanding of their subject matter. The language of hope must be analysed as carefully as the language of faith.'[13]

Already our analysis of hope has been pointing us in the direction of faith, for we have seen that any human hoping makes sense only in a world which has some measure of openness and is to some extent amenable to shaping in accordance with the goals and ideals of the human spirit. The fact that hope (and the same would be true of reason, love, faith, the pursuit of beauty and other phenomena of the spirit) has appeared in this universe of ours is itself a ground for *hoping that hope is at home in the universe*, that is to say, that the creative energy at work in the universe is itself ultimately a spiritual reality.

The point is made more explicitly and in more definitely theological language by Gordon Kaufman: 'If man could believe that the historical context into which he has been thrown were meaningful, if he could believe it to be the loving personal decision and purpose of a compassionate Father who is moving all history toward a significant goal, then anxiety would be dissolved. If he could believe his existence and decisions and actions had an indispensable place within larger purposes shaping the overall movement of history, and that even his stupid blunders and wilful perversities could be rectified and redeemed, his anxiousness and guilt could give place to confidence, creativeness and hope.'[14] Schubert Ogden draws a rather similar connection when he claims that 'logically prior to every particular religious assertion is an original confidence in the meaning and worth of life,' and when he goes on to maintain that 'the primary use or function of [the word] "God" is to refer to the objective ground in reality itself of our ineradicable confidence in the final worth of our existence.'[15]

Admittedly, of course, in all human life fear and anxiety continue to alternate with hope and confidence. But this too is entirely to be expected, for we remind ourselves again that hope is not optimism, just as faith is not knowledge. But to the extent that hope does triumph over fear, to that extent faith is overcoming doubt.

But are we not according a vastly exaggerated importance to this style of argument? Are we not trying to set up some very grand assertions on very flimsy grounds? And even if the hopes of men were taken to be evidence of some kind of religious postulate about reality, might it not all be an illusion in any case? The force of these objections has to be acknowledged, and I have already made it clear that there can be no facile transition from the fact of hope to the demonstration of the truth of faith. Clearly our everyday hopes, some of them relatively trivial but others quite important, arise within limited contexts of meaning and purpose, and are entirely explicable in these limited contexts, without appeal to some larger scheme. One is not faced with a dramatic choice between hope and despair, but one lives most of the time by limited hopes that reach so far ahead but are surrounded by areas of uncertainty and by the anxieties to which these give rise. Yet, while this is true, one has also to recognize the general predominance of hope over fear, that widespread if vague phenomenon of hopefulness form which our investigation set out, that 'original confidence in the meaning and worth of life,' to recall Ogden's phrase. The human mind is not content to deal with isolated segments of experience, but tries to put things together. Hope in particular situations tends to expand into a settled attitude of hopefulness—a hopefulness not only about one's own existence but about the humanity and the history in which that existence is set.

In modern times, many positivistic philosophers have urged us to abandon ultimate (and, as they believe, unanswerable) questions, and confine ourselves to the limited problems with which the sciences can deal. But in spite of this, man remains incurably a being with a 'sense and taste for the infinite' (Schleiermacher), a questioning being who never stops questioning no matter how far his questions may lead. He has to find an orientation for himself in the world and so he looks beyond all the limited contexts of meaning for an all-embracing context. Perhaps the most fundamental of all his hopes is to find that context. We are now in a better position to understand the sentence, 'Where there is hope, there is religion.' It draws attention to the fact that isolated hopes tend to coalesce into a unified or total hope, and it is such a total hope that implies some religious understanding of the world. It is at this point that we can do justice to Bloch's interpretation. He writes: 'If the line, "Where there is hope, there is religion," applies at all, Christianity with its vigorous starting point and its rich heretical history [of apocalyptic, revolutionary movements] seems like a final emergence of what religion is—a *total hope*, and an explosive one.'[16]

But again we come back to the limitations of the line of thought set forth in the preceding paragraphs. Hope is a fact in our world, even total hope, and as such it deserves to be taken seriously as a phenomenon which helps to interpret the world. Yet, on the other hand, hope may be illusion, especially total hope. The argument from hope cannot stand by itself, though it has a contribution to make to the wider web of arguments which together constitute the case for the truth of religion.

We have several times used the expression, 'total hope,' taken from the writings of Ernst Bloch. We have made a beginning toward the exploration of this expression. Needless to say, it is not the optimism which has been criticized above. It is genuine hope, in all its vulnerability, humility and fallibility. But it is hope that reaches out beyond particular situations of hoping to embrace life as a whole— the life of an individual or even the life of a community or of the whole human race. It may even be possible to conceive of a hope for the world itself. What gives birth to such hopes or impels people toward them?

Part of the answer to this question lies in what we have already seen of the human drive toward transcendence. But perhaps equally important is the fact of total threat, which constitutes the foil to total hope. By 'total threat,' I mean, of course, the threat of death. In the face of death, every human hope seems to wilt, for whatever may be fulfilled on this occasion or that will finally be cancelled out, and it will be as if neither hope nor promise nor fulfilment had ever been. Death, according to Sartre, 'removes all meaning from life.'[17] It destroys the context in which hope lives. From the earliest times, people have experienced death as a total threat, a phenomenon so incongruous or even absurd that they have felt it necessary to explain why human life should be afflicted with such an evil and in their myths have represented it as perhaps a divine punishment, imposed for some primeval sin.

In modern times, death has taken on vaster dimensions and we can attach more definite meaning to the expression 'total threat.' No longer is it just the death of the individual that threatens, or even genocide, terrible though that is. In the age of nuclear weapons, the demise of the whole human race has been made a possibility with which we must seriously reckon. Since 1945, we have all been living under the shadow of a threat greater than any that had been known before. Even if mankind succeeds in taming the nuclear terror (which means in effect taming himself), the threat of universal death will certainly not have been removed. For now there is the environmental threat. The using up of scarce resources, the pollution of the environment and the massive increase of the human population add up to another total threat no less frightening than the nuclear one. And even if some way is found whereby these environmental threats may be held off and some state of equilibrium attained, total death is still the ultimate prospect. For although it may be a long way off, the time is coming, so we are told, when life on earth or in any other part of the solar system will have become impossible, and eventually there may come a time when the whole galaxy or even the entire universe will have ground to a standstill as its energy is finally dissipated. Admittedly, this threat is so far off and so speculative that we can hardly feel excited about it. But it provides the appropriate backdrop for all the closer threats of death and annihilation, and these closer threats alone constitute a shattering onslaught on hope.

Yet that is only one side of the picture. Not everyone holds that death is an unmitigated evil, that it is unnatural, that it removes meaning from life, and so on. Even death is ambiguous. We talk about dying with dignity, and that would be senseless if death were entirely evil and negative. Sometimes we admire a death and even find inspiration in it—the death of Socrates and the death of Jesus are the examples which immediately come to mind. Whereas Sartre claims that death empties life of meaning, Heidegger on the contrary maintains that it is death that makes a meaningful life possible. For death sets a boundary to life, and makes it possible for a human life to constitute a finite whole.[18] On this view, life could be compared to a piece of music. If that piece of music just went on and on indefinitely, it would have no form or meaning or beauty. It derives its meaning and beauty by working out its material in a finite temporal pattern. So too a human life, lived in death awareness, develops its meaning from the responsible deployment of its resources in face of the end.

But how far do such arguments take us? Surely for every person whose death is meaningful, there are many more whose deaths are senseless, wasteful and frustrating. No *tour de force* can convert death into a good. This must certainly be conceded. Yet the fact that in some ways death is redeemable and can even contribute to the quality of a life suggests that hope is not entirely cancelled by death and that hope can persist even in the face of death. Just what that hope might be is not clear. Even in its most naive form, it could hardly be the belief that life continues uninterrupted and unchanged beyond death. That would be to refuse to treat death with seriousness. Most people do treat death with seriousness and always have done so. There has been the recognition that in some way, death has finality. Yet death has not quenched hope. Unclear though the hope may be, there always has been a hope that has stood out against death. Life has seemed stronger than death, and in face of the total threat of death there has arisen the total hope that even death can be transformed and made to contribute to life.

Just as a matter of historical fact, preoccupation with death together with a hope that transcends death have been characteristic of the human race since its emergence out of a merely animal existence. Theodosius Dobzhansky claims that 'death awareness is one of the basic characteristics of mankind as a biological species.'[19] Death awareness lends a new quality to the experience of temporal existence and in this way makes an important contribution to the emergence of the specifically human. From very early times, men disposed of their dead in such a way as to make it clear that however shadowy their understanding of the matter was, they were hoping beyond death. This was the case as early as palaeolithic times, perhaps even half a million years ago. E. O. James writes: 'Since of all the mysterious, disintegrating and critical situations with which man has been confronted throughout the ages, death appears to have been the most disturbing and devastating, it is hardly surprising that the earliest traces of religious belief and practice should centre in the cult of the dead.'[20] He goes on to describe a large number of burial sites that have been excavated. In many cases the bones were coloured with red ochre, for 'red is the colour of living health' and the practice indicates that these early human beings did not accept that death was the final annihilation. From those early times too it was already the custom to bury with the dead person objects that would be of help to him. At a later time the phenomenon of Egyptian religion shows us a culture in which the concern with death and with life beyond death was carried to the greatest lengths. To some extent, the elaborate burials, the mummification of the bodies and the provision in the tomb of all the necessities of ordinary daily life on earth simply continue and develop the ideas that had been around since prehistoric times. But, as Henri Frankfort has pointed out, new and more profound ideas of a transfiguration of the dead and of a different sphere where they lived in a new mode of existence were also beginning to arise. These new ideas may have been vague and not easily reconcilable with the simpler belief in a continuing life in the tomb, but they were moving the whole question to a new level.[21]

We do not need to trace the general history of the phenomenon of hope in the face of death, though later we shall have to study the special case of the development of hope in the Bible and in Christian tradition. For the moment, I want only to make the point that a hope transcending death has been characteristic of man from the beginning, and has been deepened and transformed in the light of growing knowledge and experience. Even today, in a secular age, people are far from a simple acceptance of death as the natural and inevitable end of human life. There are many evidences of this—Freud's exposure of the deep fear of death in individuals, the many ways in which we hush up death and conceal it in our social conventions, the recrudescence of interest in the occult, and so on.

What motivations lie behind the hope that reaches beyond death, or what considerations could show it to be a reasonable hope and not mere fantasy? Is it only wishful thinking, arising from the refusal on man's part to accept the brutal reality of his fate—namely, that death is real and final, that human existence is radically finite and contingent, that *Homo sapiens* is not privileged above the animals, but is as expendable as he has usually considered them to be? Or is it just the persistence of supersitition? Sir Edward Tylor argued that because in his dreams primitive man conversed with the dead and visited distant places, he came to believe that he possessed a soul separable from the body and able to survive bodily death. Then the question would arise whether a hope transcending death may not be today no more than 'a survival from a lower stage of thought, imposing on the credit of the higher by virtue not of inherent truth but of ancestral belief?'[22]

Let us agree that a wishful escapist thinking and a superstitious misinterpretation of such experiences as dreaming of the dead may have had much to do with the rise of hopes that reach beyond death.

No doubt these influences still play a part, especially the first of them. But it would be unfair not to recognize that in course of time new motives made themselves felt. Among them was the demand for justice—and we shall come back to this point when we consider the biblical material on the subject.[23] But there are so many cases where death cuts short a promising life or strikes down a good man or frustrates and nullifies the very opportunity to live that if there is any justice in the world, any 'Power not ourselves making for righteousness' (Matthew Arnold), then must not one hope beyond death? There is some truth in Moltmann's claim that 'resurrection of the dead was a way toward expressing belief in the righteousness of God, which cannot be limited, even by death.'[24] Again, there has been the gradual rise of the belief in the absolute worth and irreplaceability of every human soul. Does not this belief, which seems to be a main support of the recognition of human dignity and freedom, call for the further belief that persons are not annihilated by death? A further consideration arises from a characteristic of human existence to which we have already alluded more than once and which has become almost a commonplace in contemporary theories about the nature of man—the fact that at every moment of his existence, he is projecting himself ahead of himself, he is reaching out to a condition of himself which is not yet realized and yet which in another sense already is part of himself. The human being is more than he actually is, he is constituted by his possibility and not merely by his actuality. 'The human being,' declares Helmut Thielicke, 'is only to be defined in terms of his whither, not of his whence.'[25] On this view, humanity is something that is still in process of coming to be, so we have to look toward the goal if we are to understand what humanity truly is. And some would then argue that the goal lies beyond the event which we call death. Man projects himself toward a goal that transcends not only death but the conditions of finite existence in time. W. Pannenberg maintains that the phenomenological analysis of man's life as we know it shows that 'it is inherent in man to hope beyond death, even as it is inherent in man to know about his own death.'[26] What the force of this argument is, or what is the nature of the hope of which it speaks (for it would seem to be something a good deal more sophisticated than the continuation of a life much like the present one beyond death) are questions to which we shall return shortly.

But first it will be helpful to explore some of these issues more fully. I doubt if there has been a better statement of the argument that an examination of the human condition leads to positing an eternal good as the goal of man than is given by the British philosopher Alfred Edward Taylor. It will be worth our while to study his argument rather carefully.

Although he was writing in the earlier part of the present century, Taylor had already come to share the dynamic view of man that has more and more established itself—the view that man is a being who, so to speak, has not yet arrived and is still on the way to the fulfilment of what he has in him to become. It is significant that Taylor several times quotes a pioneer of this view, Nietzsche, with general approval. Thus, he mentions Nietzsche's injunction, *'Werde was du bist!'* ('Become what you are!'). Taylor comments: 'We might fairly say that Nietzsche has given the perfect expression for the supreme "categorical imperative" if only we are careful to remember from the first that I do not, from the outset, know who or what I am; I am a riddle to myself, and it is only through the process of the becoming (*Werden*) that I slowly and painfully gain some insight into my being (*Sein*).'[27] Again, he quotes Nietzsche's view that humanity is something that must be surpassed (*etwas das überwunden werden muss*), but corrects this by saying 'it is rather true that it is something that has to be *won*.'[28] The reason for this is that human life has in it the tension of two opposites, the temporal and the eternal. Man is 'a being who is neither simply eternal and abiding, nor simply mutable and temporal, but both at once; the task of living rightly and worthily is just the task of the progressive transmutation of a self which is at first all but wholly mutable, at the mercy of all the gusts of circumstance and impulse, into one which is relatively lifted above change and mutability.'[29] I think we can discern in this a view of man akin to that which we have been assuming in the preceding pages—man as a temporal being who is in a process of projection and self-transcendence, and at the same time a being with a sense and taste for the infinite.

Taylor then points out that even in ordinary experience we transcend the mere successiveness of instants, and live in a span of time which we experience all at once. For instance, this happens when one is listening to music, and grasps a musical theme or even a whole movement as a unity; or when one is listening to someone speaking, and hears not just a succession of sounds but sentences, arguments, stories. This affords a clue, however meagre, to what is meant by eternity. Eternity is not sheer timelessness. Like the human experiences mentioned, it admits a before and an after, but not a no-longer and a not-yet. Taylor quotes Boethius' famous definition of eternity: *interminabilis vitae tota simul et perfecta possessio* (the whole, simultaneous and complete fruition of a life without bounds).

The argument is that the goal of human hope and striving must have the quality of eternity, as interpreted here. Again Nietzsche is quoted: '*Alle Lust will Ewigkeit.*' 'Every enjoyment seeks to be eternal.' Man is temporal, but he is always striving to overcome the successiveness of temporal existence. Sometimes, in listening to music for instance, the mind is filled with a kind of satisfaction like that described by Boethius. But, of course, one soon has to come back to other matters. In life as we know it in our ordinary experience, 'simultaneous and complete fruition' is an ideal, not an actuality. Our satisfactions come *seriatim*, if they come at all. As far as individuals are concerned, 'we cannot have the ripe wisdom, assured judgment, and reflective serenity of maturity at its best without leaving behind the ardours and impetuosities and adventures of act which belong to youth, and these, again, you cannot have without losing much of the naive wonder, the readiness to be delighted by little things, the divine thoughtlessness of childhood.'[30] A similar argument holds for nations and cultures: 'However much we gain in the way of good by what we call advance in civilization, something which is also good has to be surrendered. Life is made more secure, but, in the course of becoming more secure, it loses its quality of adventure and becomes tame and commonplace.'[31] Taylor takes this to mean that we can never rest satisfied with secular goods. 'We can imagine a kind of life in which all our various aims and interests should be so completely unified by reference to a supreme and all-embracing good that all action had the same character of completeness which is imperfectly illustrated by our enjoyment of a musical pattern.'[32] So the argument finally comes to this, that when we consider seriously the hopes and aspirations that arise in man's temporal existence, we have to acknowledge that they can be satisfied only in an eternal mode of existence; or, to put it somewhat differently, all our seeking for the good is ultimately directed to a *summum bonum* which cannot be less than God.

What importance can we attach to this argument, which, as it seems to me, puts forward in some detail the point made rather sketchily by Pannenberg that the phenomenology of hope shows man as a being whose fulfilment must transcend death? I think that in order to judge the argument fairly, one must be careful to set beside it two qualifications.

The first is that the argument has to be understood in such a way that it is compatible with the finitude of man. I am suspicious, for instance, of Taylor's introduction of Boethius' language of the *totum simul* and the idea of the whole, simultaneous and complete fruition of a life without bounds. Is this conceivable for a finite being—even if such a being has a sense and taste for the infinite? I believe a distinction has to be made between the case of the person who, through untimely death, has been deprived of the possibility of bringing to fruition his most distinctive possibilities, and the person who has chosen to set aside some potentialities in order to develop others. The second case, as it seems to me, is precisely what finite existence requires. To use a familiar figure, we can think of the individual standing before a block of uncarved stone. That block is the sum total of his potentialities, and out of it he has to sculpt a meaningful life. He does that by his decisions, and every 'de-cision' is a cutting away; that is to say, it is a decision against as well as a decision for, it means relinquishing one possibility in order to take up another. The one reliquished may be something for which the person is very well fitted, as when he weighs two possible careers, knowing that he might have much to contribute in either of them, yet knowing also that he must choose one to the exclusion of the other. Every decision is, in a sense, a death—it is discarding something that might have been part of one's life. But this is precisely how a life, on the plane of finite existence, must be lived—and here again we are reminded that death has its affirmative aspects. To come back to our metaphor of the block of stone: the sculptor can only reveal the possibilities of that block and produce from it something harmonious, meaningful—yes, beautiful—if he chips away much of the stone. If he put all those chippings back, the shape would have disappeared and we would be back to the beginning. Must it not be so in a finite existence? It is intensity, not extendedness whether in time or in range of activities, that gives such a life its point and its worth. If all the potentialities unrealized in the finite life-span were somehow to be realized 'beyond' this life, would not the shape disappear? Would we not have, so to speak, a bloated existence, without any distinctive character? Perhaps it is reserved to God to fulfil all possibilities, but his existence is on quite another plane from ours. Perhaps too it is in God and in fellowship with each other in God that we experience vicariously the fulfilment of potentialities which we are not able to fulfil in our separate strips of existence. At any rate, the kind of questions I have raised here have to be borne in mind in appraising Taylor's argument—and, *a fortiori*, that of Pannenberg.

But a further qualification or question mark has to be raised. The argument stated by Taylor rests on a presupposition. If one accepts the presupposition, then the argument has considerable force, assuming that one can find a satisfactory way of dealing with the questions which I raised under my first qualification. But if the presupposition is not accepted, then the argument seems to be deprived of its force.

Taylor himself clearly understands the presupposition that he brings to the argument, and he had in fact already defended it in an earlier chapter of his book. That presupposition is (to use his terminology) that fact and value belong together. This means that human beings and the values after which they aspire and the highest hopes that they entertain are not foreign bodies, mere accidents or anomalies, in the universal process which has brought forth the human race, but are rather clues to the character of that process itself. If one accepts that they are clues, even our best clues, then the fact that man appears to hope beyond death is itself a good reason for believing that he has an eternal destiny. But if one thinks there are reasons for believing that the cosmic process is quite indifferent to man and to human values and moral aspirations, then human hopes and the human desire for an eternal good prove nothing, except that man is the rather pathetic victim of an illusion of grandeur. In that case, the right reaction (if there is a 'right' reaction) might be to accept Camus's invitation to 'metaphysical rebellion,' which he describes as 'the movement by which man protests against his condition and the whole of creation.'[33] The argument that if man's dearest hopes can never be fulfilled, then the universe is unjust, may simply call for the reply that the universe is indeed unjust—or, rather, knows nothing of justice or injustice.

The theist has to be very careful not to get into a circular argument at this point. If he holds that the fact of man's hoping for an eternal good (or a good that transcends death) is evidence that man has a destiny not annihilated by death, then he is already assuming some form of theism, because his argument presupposes that this is something that justice demands and so that there is a moral governance of the universe. He cannot then use the fact of hope as an argument for theism, and this would have to be established on some other ground. One might, for instance, hold that it is more plausible to believe that fact and value belong together, that man and his spiritual aspirations are of a piece with the rest of the universe, than to accept a dualistic view which sees a disjunction between the processes of nature and the life of spirit.

At various stages of our discussion we have touched on the problem of time and temporality. Even if hope aims ultimately at an eternal good, hope is very closely connected with the existence of man in time, and eternity itself (so far as we have been able to understand this idea) is not sheer timelessness. In our exploration into the nature of hope, therefore, we must consider more fully than we have done so far the relation of hope and time.

At first sight, it would seem that hope has to do primarily with that dimension of time which we call the future. The object of hope is something that lies ahead, and the hopeful person is the person who is very much aware of the future, the new, the possibilities of change and the other categories that belong especially to a hopeful understanding of life. But while this is true, hope becomes distorted if it leads to excessive preoccupation with the future. It is such preoccupation that gives birth to unrealistic and utopian hopes. We have already noted how the creative imagination in hope needs to be kept in bounds by rational criticism and realistic planning, and in temporal terms this means that any vision of the future has to be related to the hard facts of the present and the past. If this does not happen, then proliferation of false hopes and their eventual unmasking can turn hope into despair and bitterness.

But there is a still more serious ethical problem that comes from an obsession with the future. We might call it the suspension of morality in the present. I mean that the obsession with the future can lead not just to contempt for the past but to indifference toward the present. The future vision comes to be all that matters, and all else has to be sacrificed for its realization. This has been characteristic of political revolutions, and examples are to be found in the terror that followed the French revolution, the purges that came after the Russian revolution, and the persecutions that still follow in the wake of any violent revolution. All those revolutions began with a vision of a more humane future which, rightly, was employed as a critique of the prevailing inhuman conditions. But as time goes on, to the revolutionary the future alone seems real and has value, while the present is regarded only as a stage on the way to the future. It is at this point that revolutions turn inhuman. The present exists only to be surpassed, and those who live in the present are, like all else belonging to it, expendable for the sake of the supposed future good.

I am saying then that hope has to be related to the present and the past if it is to be saved from irrelevance, escapism and, at the worst, the possibility of downright inhumanity. Hope has its being in the tension of future and present, driving us out of the present, yet seeing the future from the present situation. A hope that relates only to an imagined future, whether that hope be religious or secular, is a false and alienating hope.

But hope is related to past and present experience in a more affirmative way than just as providing a touchstone for discriminating realistic from fantastic hopes. If there were no past experiences, either our own or reliably reported, of apparently 'hopeless' situations which had been resolved by the irruption of the new and the hopeful, and if there was no possibility of hope in our present experience, then we could have no hope for the future. The human self has always past, present and future dimensions, and needs all three to be genuinely a self. If a free undetermined space in the future is needed for selfhood and identity, so is a history and a tradition from the past. Where one dimension of temporality becomes so dominant that the others are brought near to elimination, selfhood is distorted, for it has fallen into a pathological condition. The person who is absorbed in the future can lose touch with reality, so that he lives in a dream world. The person who dwells in the past becomes the creature of routine and habit, afraid to face the future with its certainty of change and novelty. While of anyone absorbed in the present, it may be said that he has not really begun to achieve selfhood or personhood at all, for to be at the mercy of every passing circumstance or every transient desire is to live on the level of the animal. It is not yet to transcend the instant so as to live in a 'span' of time, which is possible only through anticipation of the future and retention of the past. But it is only at this level that one can properly speak of a self or of personal being.

Hope is a personal quality, and therefore true hope has to relate itself to all the dimensions of personal being, and this means to the present and the past as well as the future. Hope is indeed primarily directed to the future, but it must not be severed from its roots in past and present experience.

Finally, we have to remember that although our discussion of hope, if it is to be manageable, must often consider the hope of the individual person, it is equally important that we do not lose sight of what it means to hope for a community, to hope for the human race, even to hope for the cosmos. We have indeed already taken note of the other side of the coin, so to speak, the fear of a universal death or annihilation. Just as in our own time we have become acutely conscious of the total threat to mankind, so we have simultaneously been learning the solidarity of the race and that my hopes and your hopes are not independent but intermeshing at many points. A total hope cannot be just the hope that all the threats to your existence or my existence can be overcome, but that somehow the threat to existence as a whole is one that can be transcended. Every little hope is part of a larger hope. So far as the larger hopes grow out of the little hopes and are continuous with them, they are not fanciful or alienating but the natural fulfilment toward which the little hopes tend. The largest hope of all is the total hope of religion. In St. Thomas' words, 'The good we should rightly and chiefly hope for from God is an unlimited one, matching the power of God who helps us. For it belongs to his limitless power to bring us to limitless good.'[34]

Notes
[1] Karl Marx and Friedrich Engels, *On Religion* (Schocken Books, New York, 1964), p. 42.
[2] Karl Barth, *Church Dogmatics*, vol. 1/2, tr. G. T. Thompson and Harold Knight (T. & T. Clark, Edinburgh, 1956). p. 716.
[3] Ludwig Feuerbach, *The Essence of Christianity*, tr. George Eliot (Harper & Row, New York, 1957), p. 236.
[4] Gabriel Marcel, *Homo Viator: Introduction to a Metaphysic of Hope*, tr. Emma Craufurd (Victor Gollancz, London, 1951), p. 29.
[5] Thomas Aquinas, *Summa Theologiae*, vol. XXXIII, tr. William J. Hill, O.P. (Eyre & Spottiswoode, London, 1966), p. 5 (2a2ae, q. 17, a. 1).
[6] Reinhold Niebuhr, *Justice and Mercy* (Harper & Row, New York, 1974), p. v.
[7] Albert Camus, *The Rebel: An Essay on Man in Revolt*, tr. Anthony Bower (Alfred A. Knopf, New York, 1956), pp. 23, 100.
[8] Ronald Gregor Smith, *Secular Christianity* (Collins, London, 1966), p. 127.
[9] Jürgen Moltmann, *Hope and Planning*, tr. Margaret Clarkson (S.C.M. Press, London, 1971), p. 178.
[10] See below, pp. 53–55.
[11] Rubem A. Alves, *A Theology of Human Hope* (Corpus Books, Washington, 1969), p. 102.
[12] See below, p. 18.
[13] James Alfred Martin, *The New Dialogue between Philosophy and Theology* (Seabury Press, New York, 1966), p. 99.
[14] Gordon D. Kaufman, *Systematic Theology: A Historicist Perspective* (Charles Scribner's Sons, New York, 1968), p. 350.
[15] Schubert M. Ogden, *The Reality of God* (Harper & Row, New York, 1966), pp. 34, 37.

[16] Ernst Bloch, *Man on His Own: Essays in the Philosophy of Religion*, tr. E. B. Ashton (Herder & Herder, New York, 1970), p. 152.

[17] Jean-Paul Sartre, *Being and Nothingness: An Essay on Phenomenological Ontology*, tr. Hazel E. Barnes (Philosophical Library, New York, 1956), p. 539.

[18] Martin Heidegger, *Being and Time*, tr. John Macquarrie and Edward S. Robinson (Harper & Row, New York, 1962), p. 279ff.

[19] Theodosius Dobzhansky, *The Biology of Ultimate Concern* (New American Library, New York, 1967), p. 72.

[20] E. O. James, *Prehistoric Religion* (Thames & Hudson, London, 1957), p. 17.

[21] Henri Frankfort, *Ancient Egyptian Religion* (Harper & Row, New York, 1961), p. 100ff.

[22] E. B. Tylor, *Primitive Culture* (Harper & Row, New York, 1958), vol. II, p. 539.

[23] See below, p. 40.

[24] Jürgen Moltmann, *The Crucified God*, tr. R. A. Wilson and John Bowden (S.C.M. Press, London, 1974), p. 174.

[25] Helmut Thielicke, *Menschsein—Menschwerden: Entwurf einer christlichen Anthropologie* (Piper Verlag, Munich, 1976), p. 431.

[26] Wolfhart Pannenburg, *What Is Man? Contemporary Anthropology in Theological Perspective*, tr. D. A. Priebe (Fortress Press, Philadelphia, 1970), p. 44.

[27] A. E. Taylor, *The Faith of a Moralist* (Macmillan, London, 1937), vol. I, p. 68.

[28] Ibid., p. 72.

[29] Ibid., p. 69.

[30] Ibid., pp. 94–5.

[31] Ibid., p. 95.

[32] Ibid., p. 92.

[33] Albert Camus, ibid., p. 23.

[34] Thomas Aquinas, ibid., p. 9 (2a2ae, q. 17, a. 2).

II
The Hope of Israel

It was the prophet Jeremiah who addressed God as 'Thou hope of Israel!' (Jer. 14, 8). It would be difficult indeed to imagine a more apposite title for Israel's Lord. Perhaps we are more accustomed to think of him as a God of righteousness and as the God who gave Israel a law. But, as St. Paul declares, he was first a God of hope, and promise had priority over law: 'Now the promises were made to Abraham and to his offspring . . . The law, which came four hundred and thirty years afterward, does not annul a covenant previously ratified by God, so as to make the promise void' (Gal. 3, 16–17). So any discussion of the faith of Israel can confidently assume as a fundamental datum that for Israel God and hope stand in the closest association—indeed, they are almost identified.

It is natural then that we should attend to Israel's experience of hope as an outstanding manifestation of the place of hope, even of total hope, in a segment of actual human history. I do not intend to give a summary of the role of hope in the Old Testament or its place in the context of biblical theology, but to select for discussion three important themes that have a bearing on hope in the biblical tradition, and to use these in order to give depth and content to the view of hope that was set out in the first chapter. That was based mainly on a consideration of hope as we know it in general human experience, and of the implications which can be drawn from this apparently universal human attitude. But now we have to bring these general human phenomena into a more direct confrontation with the biblical revelation so that we can see them in a new concreteness derived from the history of hope in that revelation.

There are three topics to which we shall devote special attention. The first is the nature of eschatology, and the ways in which it developed and became elaborated in the Hebrew-Jewish tradition. The second is the change in the consciousness of time which accompanies the rise of eschatology; and it will be shown that this is a change which is still going on at the present time. The third topic will be the promise-fulfilment schema which, as some theologians have claimed, forms the framework for the Old Testament exposition of history and which is so important for our general theme that it must be subjected to a particularly close critical scrutiny.

1. *Eschatology*

We begin then with eschatology. The form of the word shows that it is a branch of study. More particularly, it is a branch of theological study. The term, which is a relatively modern one, indicates that branch of theology which considers the doctrine of the *eschata* or 'last things.' Immediately, of course, an ambiguity discloses itself. The 'last things' may be the things that come along at the end of a series, and here 'last' has primarily a temporal significance. Yet, since it is what closes a series that gives to it any meaning or character it may have, the 'last things' may also be understood as what is final and ultimate, what is of most importance; and in some modern theologians (Bultmann and Tillich are examples) the eschatological is virtually voided of any temporal reference and is understood as the ultimate or decisive moment. The ambiguity is not removed but takes on a somewhat different meaning if we substitute the language of 'end' for that of 'last things.' For the 'end' may be understood as the finish, the stopping place of the series, and there are nowadays various secular speculations about an end to history and some of these would visualize it as simply a finish, perhaps even a quite incongruous finish to what has gone before. On the other hand, the 'end' may be understood as goal and fulfilment, and clearly this is implied in the biblical view. The 'end' will be God's consummation of the work which he began in creation. Once more, however, if we concentrate attention on the ideas of completion and fulfilment, the temporal reference of 'end' may be dimmed down or even eliminated, for we can see that just as creation might be understood in terms of a continuous creativity rather than an initial act, so consummation could be understood as a continuous work of completing and perfecting rather than a final moment.

But however we may interpret the expressions 'last things' and 'end,' to have become concerned with these rather than with first things and beginnings was quite a revolution in the history of religion. The nature of this revolution has been well expounded by Mircea Eliade. The function of religion was to maintain a certain stability, and this it did by bringing again, in its myths and rituals, the archetypal events of the beginning. It established 'an ontology uncontaminated by time or becoming.'[1] Events were supposed to move in cycles which kept on repeating themselves. But with the rise of eschatology, that archaic way of understanding events was broken up. As soon as men began to look forward to an end as well as backward to a beginning, to last things as well as to first things, they were already in process of being expelled from the paradise of recurring archetypes. To be sure, the old beliefs would prove to be stubbornly persistent and would seek to come back in new forms, but they had been in principle undermined. The human race had begun to learn that its history is irreversible and unrepeatable.

Ancient Iranian religion is often cited by historians as the matrix within which the eschatological outlook first came into being, but the question of origins is not important from the point of view of our own study. Wherever eschatology may have been born, it achieved its most profound and influential development in the biblical tradition. The history contained in the Hebrew scriptures is a history written toward the future, and this is true from the very earliest chapters of this history. Of course, I do not mean that there was a consciously eschatological expectation throughout the whole of that history. Obviously, the history as we have it is an idealized one and is told by those who view it in retrospect and in the light of their own expectations. It is from their relatively sophisticated point of view that, for instance, the story of Abraham is told as the story of a response to a promise, as a quest for a new mode of existence to be sought in the unformed wilderness rather than in the cities already determined by their past. Yet when the Old Testament historians understood the past of their nation in such ways, they were surely not imposing an alien pattern upon it or doing violence to it, any more than the Christian theologian in turn does violence to the work of these same Hebrew writers when he interprets what they have written as an 'Old Testament' and seeks to understand it in the light of the New Testament. In all such cases, the interpretation of the events is from the end, and from that vantage point they are bound to look very different from the way they looked from the beginning or when they were actually going on. We shall have to consider this more carefully when we come to the questions of time-consciousness and of the adequacy of the promise-fulfilment schema.

The new outlook came to be extended even beyond the earliest history of the people to the origins of the world itself, that is to say, to the doctrine of creation. According to Von Rad, the Old Testament doctrine of creation is essentially different from the myths of creation which abound in the religions of the Near East. The difference lies in the fact that Israel 'learned to see creation as connected theologically with the saving history.'[2] Again, of course, this was something that came about over a period of time, and Israel had no doubt originally its creation myths very little different from those of other archaic peoples, and traces of them remain in the Old Testament. But in retrospect these are incorporated into the new historical understanding. Von Rad's speculation does have an inherent plausibility. It would be in limited segments of experience that a people or a group within a people would first glimpse the understanding of history as having a meaning, an order and goal. Then the interpretation of the limited segment would be applied to wider areas and finally to creation itself. In the mythical mentality described by Eliade, there was posited at the beginning a 'golden age,' and subsequent events (one could scarcely speak of 'history') were understood as a decline or falling away from the original paradise; though no doubt the circling of the times would bring back that golden age, and the religious celebration of the archetypes gave assurance of that. The biblical story of creation does indeed include the story of a fall, but the fall is linked with a prediction of the conflicts of history and the triumph of the seed of the woman over the serpent: 'I will put enmity between you and the woman, and between your seed and her seed; he shall bruise your head, and you shall bruise his heel' (Gen. 3, 15). The early Christian theologians delighted to see in these words a *protevangelium*, a primitive announcement of the gospel. And again we may say that from their vantage point, their interpretation was a legitimate one. Everything gets turned around, as in Hegel's dialectic where everything tends to pass over into its opposite: Eva becomes *Ave*, the tree of the garden becomes the tree of the cross, and so on. The point is that both Hebrew and Christian theologians bring the myths of creation into history, and set them in the interim between promise and fulfilment. When thought through to the end, the idea of creation must become that of an ongoing process inseparable from redemption and consummation, rather than an isolated event at the beginning. This understanding is reached through the experience of a limited tract of history that is taken to be revelatory. But what has come first in the order of knowing is held to be derivative in the order of being, and so may serve as a clue to the nature of all history and all creation. As such a clue or paradigm, it is called 'revelation.'

The inclusion of creation within the purview of an eschatologically oriented history is important both because it can be understood as ontologically grounding this conception of history in the very nature of things and because it provides the possibility of attaining to the idea of a cosmic eschatology. But we come back meanwhile to history.

As we have already seen, that history begins concretely with Abraham. He makes a break with the settled past, by turning his back on the cities of Mesopotamia, and ventures into the new, in quest of a community and a destiny. At least, this is how his descendants came to understand the matter. How he himself understood it, we cannot know, but there would seem to be no reason why we should deny to him the title of the 'first man of faith,' conferred by later generations—though perhaps it would be nearer the truth to see him as the leader of the first community of faith. Much of the rest of the Old Testament is taken up with the subsequent history of this community, and we find it has the same forward-looking character. The exodus of the tribes from Egypt, again into the unformed wilderness, is something like a repetition of the original exodus of Abraham from the city. I do not mean this in the sense that a new kind of cycle is being set up to replace the one from which Abraham had emerged, for there is surely novelty and irreversibility in these acts of exodus. But the looking forward to an end needs to be renewed from time to time. Then follows the pilgrimage to the promised land, the excitement of conquest and the founding of a new state, the expectations associated with it and, even after the state had disappeared as a political entity, the new expectations of return and restoration. It was in the course of living this history that Israel developed an understanding of its history which both provided a framework for the telling of that history and, we may say, became itself a part of the history of Israel. The gradual deepening and elaboration of Israel's understanding of its own history during the undergoing of that history led to the emergence of a number of new ideas which are very important for our theme of hope.

First among them we may mention the messianic expectation. Strictly speaking, a 'messiah' is an anointed person, and originally there were no future connotations associated with the word. Saul and David were anointed to be kings over Israel, and indeed it might well have seemed that with the establishment of the kingdom and then later with the building of the Temple in Solomon's time, the hopes of the nation were being realized. But the golden age of the Hebrew monarchy was shortlived. The kingdom split apart, foreign invaders harassed the people from without, while within there were apostasies and injustices. So again attention moves to the future, to a time of promise when hopes will be fulfilled. These hopes become focused on a messiah or anointed one, an ideal ruler of the house of David who will bring in a reign of peace, prosperity, justice and true religion. Scholars are divided on the question of the time at which such a hope emerged and also on the exegesis of those passages which are claimed as messianic. But it is generally agreed that some such messianic expectation had a place in the teaching of the classic Hebrew prophets, especially Isaiah, Micah, Jeremiah and Ezekiel. Isaiah's assurances of the coming of an ideal ruler (see, for instance, Is. 9, 2–7 and 11, 1–9) are probably the best known, but they also show the difficulty of making a true exegesis, for these passages have become so inextricably bound up with the Christmas story that it has become impossible for Christians to hear them without bringing along all the connotations and interpretations that have gathered around them.

Nevertheless, we can see in these messianic expectations an important form of that eschatological hope which came to be distinctive of the biblical understanding of history. Indeed, it may well have been with the emergence of the messianic expectation that this understanding of history began to take definite form, for we have noted that the earlier history, from Abraham to the Davidic kingdom, had been idealized by those who narrated it many centuries later.

One might ask why the eschatological hope came to be associated with a messiah or prince, that is to say, with an individual figure, rather than with the community as a whole. I think there are more ways than one of answering this question. Firstly, one cannot really separate the ruler and his people (any more than one could separate Abraham from his community), for each implies the other. But, secondly, the focusing of expectations on the anointed ruler is in line with the particularity and concreteness of the Old Testament. The eschatological hope was never a *theory* of history or some abstract philosophical idea about how things happen. As we have stressed above, it developed out of an experience of history, and found expression not in general propositions about history but in concrete assertions about this or that particular happening. This means too that the messianic expectation was, at least in its beginnings, thoroughly this-worldly. Sometimes, indeed, one might detect in the language of the prophets something of the 'golden age' mythology— 'a time of idyllic, Eden-like peace,' as John Bright has expressed it,[3] when wild animals would lie down with tame ones (Is. 11, 6–7) and the desert would flourish luxuriantly (Is. 35, 1–2). But apart from such poetic touches, the expectation was a thoroughly realistic one: a time of justice, good government, freedom from oppression, a time of plenty, good crops, harmony and peace.

It is important to notice too that from the beginning the messianic hope or expectation was a dialectical one. In depended upon a promise or covenant by which God had committed himself to his people, but the people too had their responsibility arising from the covenant, and they had to fulfil that responsibility if the promise was to be realized. This dialectical note is found in all the great prophets, but again it is convenient to point to Isaiah as an exemplar. About him, Eichrodt says that 'he connects the happy assurance of Yahweh's intervention on behalf of his people inseparably with the profoundly serious reality of the judgment which must threaten the people so favoured' and thus he frees the ideal rule which he envisages 'from the egotistic limitations of national self-interest.'[4] This close connection between hope and judgment cannot be too strongly stressed. In the first chapter, I went out of my way to emphasize the difference between hope and optimism,[5] and now we come to the biblical ground of that distinction. The messianic kingdom is not guaranteed by a doctrine of progress or a theory of evolution. It is no automatic result toward which events must inevitably move. The day on which righteousness would be established would *ipso facto* be the day on which all unrighteousness would be judged. 'For the Lord of hosts has a day against all that is proud and lofty, against all that is lifted up and high' (Is. 2, 12). This note of judgment is nothing different from the vision of hope. It is simply the other side of the single reality. To cherish a hope is not to escape into dream and fantasy. It is, as we have seen, to embrace that which is difficult but possible to attain—possible because there is a righteous God at work in the world. It is this God himself who is the 'hope of Israel'.

The exposition of eschatology given above is based on the classic teaching of the great Old Testament prophets, and has been chiefly illustrated from Isaiah, one of the greatest of these prophets. It was a bold forward-looking attitude, bringing both encouragement and responsibility. But in course of time the classic religion of the Old Testament passed into Judaism, and a profound change took place in the eschatological expectations of the people. Perhaps this was due to the apparent falsification by events of the original expectations. No ideal ruler appeared. On the contrary, the nation was scattered and its central institutions, the monarchy and the Temple, were destroyed. The realistic (even political) hope for an ideal kingdom seemed no longer possible of attainment. So we find that eschatology turns into apocalyptic. This-worldly expectations are superseded by new expectations with a definitely other-worldly character. Questions about individual destinies arise, whereas one had thought hitherto about the people as a whole. The difficult idea of resurrection makes its appearance. We must now give our attention to these developments, all of which had important consequences for Christian eschatology.

Eschatology, we have said, turned into apocalyptic. I am using the word 'eschatology' as a generic term for any view of history which tries to see the course of events in the light of an end or goal, whether that goal is itself taken to be within history or beyond it. Thus I have felt it proper to use the word 'eschatology' with reference to the this-worldly expectations of the classical Hebrew prophets—though, of course, these expectations were to be realized through the action of God in history. But when one speaks of 'apocalyptic,' while we are still dealing with an eschatological outlook, this is an eschatology of a highly specific character. Some people indeed might even want to restrict the term 'eschatology' to the apocalyptic type, but this would surely be an unwarranted limiting of the more general term. By its etymology, 'apocalyptic' has to do with revelations, more particularly, with revelatory visions of the future. What is distinctive in apocalyptic when contrasted with the older type of eschatology is that the whole supernatural element is stressed to a far greater extent. That element was never lacking, for, as we have noted above, it was God's action in history that was to realize the ideals of the prophets. The older prophets too had visions that might well be described as revelatory. But increasingly the stress comes to be laid on God's action independently of any human contribution, and increasingly too the language is a highly symbolic one drawn from vision and fantasy. At the same time, the end is understood as transhistorical and other-worldly. The messianic kingdom would not be a restoration or renewal of the kingdom of David, but a completely new age. It would be discontinuous rather than continuous with present history. There could be no gradual growth toward it, for it would come as a revolutionary irruption through divine power into the present age. Likewise the agent who would carry out this work on behalf of God would be no merely human person, not even a natural descendant of the house of David, but a supernatural angelic or even quasi-divine being. Some scholars have interpreted the mysterious figure of the 'Son of Man' in this way, though there is no clear agreement.

Whether such developments came about because of the disappointment of the earlier hopes is a question at which we shall have to look more closely and critically when we come to discuss the validity of the promise-fulfilment schema in the Old Testament.[6] But certainly it was in the time after the destruction of Jerusalem and the scattering of the nation, when hopes of a political consummation had pretty well foundered, that the apocalyptic literature began to flourish. The Book of Daniel, probably written in the early part of the second century before Christ, is generally reckoned as the beginning of Jewish apocalyptic literature, and has, of course, its place in the Old Testament canon. For about three hundred years, that is to say, right into Christian times, literature of this kind continued to be produced, though most of it did not attain the status of the canonical writings. It did, however, profoundly influence the mentality prevailing at the time when Christianity came into existence.

Contemporaneous with the rise of apocalyptic, we find an interest in the destiny of the individual. The older eschatology was conceived in corporate or collective terms. It was the nation of Israel that was to be renewed and was to enjoy the blessings of the messianic kingdom. It is true that already among the classical prophets there was developing the idea of personal responsibility before God and the belief that the individual could not simply hide, as it were, in the collective existence of the nation. According to R. H. Charles, Jeremiah was the first to conceive religion clearly as including the communion of the individual soul with God.[7] In course of time, this was bound to raise the question about the destiny of the individual. In classical Hebrew belief, the individual's career ended with his death. There might indeed be some vague shadowy existence in Hades or Sheol, but this would be only some minimal level of existence, and apparently cut off from God. 'Dost thou work wonders for the dead? Do the shades rise up to praise thee? Is thy steadfast love declared in the grave, or thy faithfulness in Abaddon? Are thy wonders known in the darkness, or thy saving help in the land of forgetfulness?' (Ps. 88, 10–12). And if God is unable to do anything for the dead, then conversely: 'The dead do not praise the Lord, nor any that go down into silence' (Ps. 115, 17). But if it came to be believed that there is a bond of communion between God and the individual soul, then could that simply be obliterated by death?

Characteristically, it needed a concrete case to raise this question in an acute way, and the case arose in the intertestamental period when apocalyptic ideas were proliferating. The occasion was the Maccabean wars. What was to be the destiny of those, especially the young, who died at the hands of the oppressors of the Jewish nation? We find a clearly expressed belief that God will renew the life of his witnesses: 'The king of the universe will raise us up to an everlasting renewal of life, because we have died for his laws' (2 Macc. 7, 9). It was in the same period that prayers for the dead were being offered (2 Macc. 12, 43–45). What is perhaps of special interest is that these nascent beliefs in a fuller rather than a minimal existence for the departed were motivated not by any egotistical desire to prolong the existence of oneself—the motive that is so often alleged to be the ground of such beliefs—but by the simple demand for justice that is typical of Hebrew religion throughout its history. It is worth noting too that the question was raised for the most part about young men who had never had an opportunity to fulfil their possibilities, so that it has nothing whatever to do with what we have earlier called a 'bloated' existence.[8] Of course, it might be argued that some of those young men, especially some of those who are described as having bravely undergone terrible martyrdom for the sake of their faith, lived so intensely and with such dedication in the manner of their deaths that even in that they fulfilled all the possibilities of a fully human existence. This raises difficult considerations, and we shall have to give the matter further thought when we come to reflect on the death and resurrection of Jesus Christ.

The last point of which we have to take note here is the emergence of a belief in resurrection. It is remarkable that the idea of resurrection hardly appears in the Old Testament, yet it has a central place in the New Testament where the resurrection of Jesus from the dead is the very heart of the kerygma. We have seen already that in ancient Hebrew religion there appeared to be only the belief in some shadowy minimal type of existence after death. Admittedly, we have Ezekiel's vision of the dead bones of the slain army being clothed again with flesh and coming to life (Ez. 37). But this would appear to be figurative language and to refer to the revival of the nation through a new covenant relation with God. The typical Old Testament view, as we have seen, was that the dead are withdrawn from any relation to God. Perhaps then it was chiefly a deepening conception of God that led to a belief in the possibility of a continuing relation with him and eventually to belief in resurrection. While I quoted above[9] two psalms that seem to put the dead beyond any communion with God, this may be contrasted with another psalm, whose writer declares: 'If I make my bed in Sheol, thou art there!' (Ps. 139, 9). This psalm does in fact recognize that God's presence and rule extend everywhere.

It was, of course, in the intertestamental period that belief in resurrection really established itself. Even by New Testament times, the belief was by no means universal among the Jews. In the New Testament itself, we read of the Sadducees, those conservative Jews who clung firmly to the ancient form of their faith and would not countenance such new-fangled and unscriptural ideas as that of a resurrection of the dead. But the belief was gaining ground, and passed into Christianity.

Why was it a belief in resurrection that emerged in the biblical tradition, rather than a belief in the immortality of the soul, such as one finds rising in ancient Greece when men were no longer satisfied with the Hades of the Homeric world, similar in a general way to the Sheol of the Old Testament? Is a belief in resurrection not more primitive, and harder to defend philosophically, than a belief in immortality? Admittedly, there are traces of a belief in immortality in some of the apocryphal writings that betray Greek influence. But the typical biblical belief is in resurrection, and, whatever the difficulties, it is with resurrection that we have to come to terms if we are staying within the Judeo-Christian tradition. I think we can say in the first place that resurrection commended itself rather than immortality because the biblical doctrine of creation is free from any kind of dualism. The whole creation, visible and invisible, proceeds from the one God; and likewise the human being, within that creation, is a unity, deriving both his body and his life-principle from God. Wherever one finds a doctrine of immortality of the soul, there is usually also a dualism and in particular a devaluation of the material. In the second place, belief in resurrection speaks of a fullness of existence that contrasts with what we have called the 'minimal' existence of Sheol. It is no mere shade that is going to transcend death, but a fully personal being, and in all our experience, a fully personal being is an embodied being, for only so can there be relations with a world and with other persons. These are two very good reasons for holding that a belief in resurrection is much more adequate than belief in the immortality of the soul. And they also suggest that belief in resurrection may not be so primitive or naive as it seems at first sight. Perhaps originally it was believed that this physical body of flesh and blood is reconstituted, that there literally takes place something like what Ezekiel saw in his vision of the valley of dry bones. But 'body' does not mean simply an organism of flesh, blood, bone and so on; it means also the way in which we are inserted into a world and a society, so perhaps there could be many kinds of 'bodies.' By the time we come to Paul, belief in resurrection is certainly not crude or simple-minded, but very subtle and sophisticated. But we shall return to the distinctive New Testament beliefs about resurrection later.[10]

2. A Change in the Consciousness of Time

The second topic announced for treatment in this chapter is the change in the consciousness of time that accompanied the rise of the eschatological outlook. This is something more difficult to pin down than the eschatological ideas considered in the last section. We were able to derive these fairly directly from the Old Testament and later Jewish writings. But only an indirect approach is possible when we ask about a change in the consciousness of time. Given the testimony of Israel to a shift in interest from the past toward the future, we have to try to fill in imaginatively what this implies for an awareness of time and history. Of course, we must not suppose that some great change of consciousness took place once and for all. The change itself took place over a long period—indeed, I have suggested at the beginning of this chapter that the change may still be going on. Elements of the old consciousness survived alongside the new, and from time to time they may have regained strength. If, for instance, one contrasts the religion of the Old Testament as historical religion with the pagan religions of the Near East as nature religions, and if one further associates with the first a linear conception of history and with the second a cyclic conception, one must also note that the linear and cyclic are not just opposed, but tend to come together in new combinations. For instance, the exodus from Egypt may be regarded from one point of view as the great once-for-all experience of liberation in the history of Israel, the unrepeatable moment that launched the people into a truly historical and free existence. Yet this unique moment is then captured in the ceremonies of the Passover, to be repeated from year to year. 'You shall observe this rite as an ordinance for you and for your sons for ever ... And when your children say to you, "What do you mean by this service?" you shall say, "It is the sacrifice of the Lord's passover"' (Ex. 12, 24–27). It could not be otherwise. Human nature is such that faith and dedication need to be renewed. Just as in the nature religions there were recurring festivals relating to the seasons, so in the historical religions there are also recurring festivals, repeating whatever is repeatable in the great formative moments in the history of the community. I say, 'repeating what is repeatable,' and perhaps these words call for comment. Repetition seems to be an essential constituent in an ordered, meaningful human existence, whether we are thinking of a community or an individual. An historical event is certainly in one sense unique and unrepeatable. Yet man's constitution as an historical being is such that when an event is significant for him because it discloses new dimensions or new possibilities of his being, it is possible to recall that event in such a way that it becomes once again present in something like its original power. This is more than just a remembering of what is past. It is a true re-presenting.

I gave as an example the Jewish celebration each year of the passover, and festivals of the same kind abound in Christianity. The great once-for-all events of history, Christ's birth, death and resurrection, are incorporated into what we frankly call the 'cycle' of the Christian Year, and are recalled again and again. Furthermore, the Christian sacraments are also ways of re-presenting the saving work of Christ, so that successive generations of Christians may participate in it. The underlying tension of the linear and cyclic views is illustrated from the controversies that have gone on over the question of the eucharistic sacrifice. Protestants have laid great stress on the 'once-for-allness' of Christ's sacrifice, the 'one oblation of himself once offered.' As a consequence, however, they have tended to think of

Christ's work as lying in the past, and so of the eucharist as a mere memorial. Catholics, while today they might eschew the word 'repetition,' have nevertheless thought of the eucharist as a making present of Christ's work, which is not tied to a moment of time. For Bultmann, not only the sacraments but every occasion of proclaiming the kerygma is a kind of re-presenting of the saving events. Easter, for him, is not an event of 33 AD or thereby, but the event that occurs now when the word is proclaimed and heard in faith. 'Always in your present lies the meaning in history, and you cannot see it as a spectator but only in your responsible decisions. In every moment slumbers the possibility of being the eschatological moment.'[11] It does seem to me that here we have a highly misleading use of the word 'eschatological,' for it has nothing to do with being last in a linear series but speaks of a moment that comes again and again. But Bultmann is just pushing to an extreme length that convergence of the linear and the cyclic which has its roots far back in the biblical tradition.

The point may be illustrated further from the extraordinary influence which Platonism exercised on both Judaism and Christianity. The influence of Plato was being already strongly felt in Judaism before New Testament times, and that influence reached its climax in the Christianity of the first few centuries. But how could this have been possible? Surely the understanding of time that we find in Plato is as different as could be from the understanding that is brought about by the eschatological outlook of the Bible.

It would, I think, be fair to say that Plato's understanding of time is a subtle philosophical expression of the same understanding that underlies the mythical archetypes described by Eliade. For Plato too, the realities are timeless, unchanging, the eternal ideas. Time and history have, by comparison, a lesser reality. Time, in the famous phrase, is the 'moving image of eternity.'[12] Becoming lies somewhere between being and nothing, somewhere between the real and the unreal. What we encounter in time and history is only an image of the reality, or even an image of an image, like the shadows of puppets seen on the wall of a cave and taken for reality by prisoners who have never seen anything else.[13]

Obviously, such a philosophy, in which time and becoming are believed to be in large part illusory, is in sharp contrast to the biblical belief that it is in time and history that the truths of God are revealed; and, incidentally, it is in equally sharp contrast with the modern empirical temperament for which reality is event, process, becoming, and not some static being beyond time. We come back to the question, then, how could Platonism, in spite of this very fundamental difference, have entered into an alliance with biblical thought?

The answer may simply be that there are elements of truth in both of these contrasted understandings of time and history. If it was gain when the Hebrews came out from the timelessness of mythology into the flux of a history with an end as well as a beginning, yet they could not have tolerated a pure flux of becoming, a wilderness with no features whatsoever. The stability of being is needed alongside the dynamism of becoming, and there cannot be passage from sheer novelty to novelty without the order provided by repetition, that is to say, by the re-presenting of that which has been known in the past to have power. We have seen how both Judaism and Christianity have provided for this in their cults.

The reason for this lies further back, in the very basic fact that every human being and every human community lives in the tension of a past and a future. Much evidence suggests that to begin with, it is the past that is chiefly influential. The centre of gravity, so to speak, in our consciousness of time lies in the past. But then a shift may come about, and that centre of gravity is displaced into the future. If we think of our own lives, then as children there was a kind of timelessness about experience. As we get older, the thought of the end becomes stronger, and along with this preoccupation with the future. If we think of primitive communities, their religious beliefs are marked by the timelessness of archetypal repetition. But that may give way (and, in the case of biblical religion, did give way) to an eschatological turning to the future and perhaps even to an apocalyptic preoccupation with the future. We could even venture the generalization that in the classic period of Western culture, people still lived for the most part in the undisturbed order expressed in the Platonist philosophy, while in modern times the shift has been to process, becoming, even revolution, so that we are now in the condition that Alvin Toffler calls 'future shock'—a state in which the familiar archetypes have disappeared in an overload of novelty.[14]

One could also say that time moves faster as the centre of gravity of one's time consciousness is displaced toward the future. Again, this can be illustrated from both individual existence and from the history of communities. For a child, still emerging from timelessness, a summer vacation seems to stretch endlessly, while for the middle-aged and elderly the years rush past. A religious community that is deeply conscious of eternal order dwells itself in unchanging stability, while one that has been seized by apocalyptic ideas and is looking for 'the day' lives with a sense of urgency, for everything around is perishing.

Of course, there is something pathological both in being fixated on the past and in being obsessed with the future. The more truly personal he becomes, the more a human being is able to gather in a single span his past, present and future. Where the centre of gravity lies too much in the past, his life is dominated by familiar ritual and routine and by fear of change. But where that centre of gravity has moved too far into the future, he becomes a dreamer and may even lose touch with reality altogether. So it is with political societies and religious communities. Some become fossilized through endless repetition and re-enactment of the past. Others get lost in utopianism and revolution as they plunge into an unreal and impracticable future. Obsession with the future can be just as alienating as obsession with heaven or the other-worldly, unless the vision of the future is firmly related to the experience of the past and present.

So when we consider more closely the new consciousness of time that emerges in the pages of the Old Testament, a consciousness which is oriented toward the future but which in its cult repeats the great moments of the past, we see that it is more complicated than it might appear at first sight. Israel finds its identity both by committing itself to a future and by accepting its past, and understands its present in the light of both. We might compare with this some of the emerging communities of the present time. The black community of the United States, for instance, finds its identity on the one hand through an opening toward the future, a liberation into a clear space where freedom and hope are possible. Yet even as this new possibility has opened up, there has come about a heightened awareness of the past, a new interest in black history and black culture, stretching back to the achievements of the kingdom of Benin and other early African societies.

Certainly, neither in individual nor in corporate existence can there be a nice balancing of the inheritance of the past and the thrust into the future. Attending again to the history of Israel, there were times of complacent acceptance of a heritage, contrasted with the lurid apocalypticism of late Judaism, together with many intermediate positions. Likewise in the Christian Church, though it was born in eschatology and apocalyptic, there were the Middle Ages dominated by a Platonist sense of eternity but sometimes deeply disturbed by new upsurges of the apocalyptic vision. The dialectic has continued down to our own time. At the present day, the centre of gravity has moved decisively toward the future, but if we are willing to learn from Israel and from the entire Judeo-Christian tradition, it will be clear to us that obsession with the future can be very dangerous if we do not maintain some realistic consciousness of the past.

3. *The Promise–Fulfilment Schema*

Jürgen Moltmann has claimed that theologians have been too much preoccupied with the category of revelation, understood as the giving of the knowledge of God, and too little with the category of promise; or, to express the matter more accurately, they have failed to relate sufficiently their understanding of revelation with the idea of the promises of God. 'God reveals himself,' says Moltmann, 'in the form of promise and in the history that is marked by promise. This confronts systematic theology with the question whether the understanding of divine revelation by which it is governed must not be dominated by the nature and trend of the promise.'[15] He goes on to draw a contrast between the kind of revelation that is given in the form of promise and what he calls the 'epiphany religions,' that is to say, those ways of understanding revelation which lack an eschatological dimension and think of the knowledge of God as something static and already given.

This plea for the primacy of promise as an interpretative category has certainly to be taken seriously, and at the beginning of this chapter the apostle Paul was quoted as asserting that promise is more fundamental than law in the religion of Israel.[16] One can see that the idea can be applied very widely in reading the Old Testament. After the fall, the promise is made to Eve that her seed will bruise the serpent's head ... After the flood, the promise is made to Noah (and, indeed, to all creation) that seedtime and harvest will not fail ... To Abraham comes the promise that makes him break with the past and seek a new future, the promise that he would found a great nation ... And so it goes on, and we come to the messianic promises, and the Old Testament looks forward to the New.

Yet there are also many difficulties about this promise–fulfilment schema. Moltmann is too uncritical in his acceptance of it, too mythological in his understanding of promise, and too one-sided in his preference for this style of interpretation as against others. It is significant that W. Pannenberg, who once shared Moltmann's enthusiasm for this schema, has withdrawn from any straightforward adherence to it. I have myself been critical of Moltmann's preoccupation with the promise–fulfilment schema and have sought to raise questions about the meaning of promise and fulfilment language which Moltmann himself has failed to raise. Nevertheless, when these questions have been raised, I believe we can find our way to establishing some measure of validity for the promise–fulfilment schema. Within limits, it can be a helpful way of interpreting God's action. The critical questions that have to be asked are as follows. What is a promise generally, and, more specifically, what is a promise of God? Can such a promise be understood in a way that is not crudely anthropomorphic? How is such a promise of God communicated and recognized? Can we point to any instances of such promises having been fulfilled? How do we know that a promise of God has been fulfilled? Alternatively, is there any way of knowing that a promise (or what was taken to be a promise) has not been fulfilled? Can one ever point to events which have falsified a promise of God?

I suppose that a promise is an example of performative language, that is to say, a use of language which does not merely state or describe or convey information, but actually *does* something. A promise binds the person who makes it to do something or give something or bring about some state of affairs in the future. A promise is usually made to some other person or persons, though one can also make a promise to oneself. Where the promise is made to another, he too is involved in it. If he accepts the promise, he hopes for its fulfilment, and we have seen that hope is not just a passive waiting, for it is a total attitude including will. At the very least, while the promiser pledges or binds himself to bring about a state of affairs, the promisee assents to that projected state of affairs and implicitly pledges his co-operation in helping to bring it about. In some cases, something more may be demanded. The promise may be conditional: 'I promise to do this, if you do that.'

It is worth noting that there is no distinct word meaning 'to promise' in the Hebrew of the Old Testament. People simply 'say' (though presumably in a solemn way) that they will perform such and such an action. This makes clear the performative character of promise language, to which I have already drawn attention. The uttering of the words is already the beginning of the act. But while there is no special word for promise, the Old Testament makes much of the idea of 'covenant,' and this is closely related. The reciprocity of the relationship is very clear in a covenant. While indeed one of the parties initiates the covenant and may take the major obligation on himself, the other party too has accepted an obligation. The relation, again, is not merely legalistic, as if it consisted only in performing certain actions, but it is constituted also by the inward loyalty of the parties to each other. This would seem to be important in the relation set up by a promise or any analogous pledge. If we were to use the terminology of a modern philosopher, Gabriel Marcel, we could say that the parties to a promise or a covenant 'engage' themselves, and such engagement rests in turn on a basic 'fidelity' which is essential to human community and personality.

Perhaps these remarks clarify somewhat the nature of the promises that are being continually made among human beings, but do they help at all with the much more mysterious notion of a 'promise of God'? Does God really make promises, as the Bible seems to suggest? In the Old Testament God actually speaks words to Eve, Noah, Abraham, Moses or whoever it may be, but although this is how the biblical writers represent it, we can hardly think of God as literally speaking to these people or literally making promises in the way that goes on among human beings. Can we reach any more satisfactory understanding of what might be meant by a promise of God?

Could we think of it in some such way as follows? Human beings find themselves existing on this earth. They did not create themselves or their earth, they do not know where they have come from or why they (or anything) should exist at all, indeed, they do not even quite know what it means to entertain such questions. But they not only exist. They exist with some understanding of themselves, and some understanding of what they can become. We could say that they exist with a conscience. Or we could say that they exist with a sense of vocation—the vocation in the first instance simply to become more fully persons in a community of persons, though each one will then have to spell out this vocation in the specific terms of his or her own unique existence. Now, when we speak of conscience or vocation, we are introducing also the notion of obligation. Conscience and vocation are felt as a constraint upon me—the constraint to become what I *can* become.

But to have a conscience, to become aware of a vocation even in the broadest (though also the most fundamental) sense, to be laid under an obligation, to experience a constraint that is not from outside but is given with my very existence as a human being—all this is also to become aware of a promise. It is a promise that is carried within human existence itself. Human existence is not something fixed. It begins as a promise of becoming that which it can become, but has not yet become. But why do we say a promise? Behind this lies the Kantian *dictum* that ought implies can. An obligation, a vocation, a constraint—these make no sense unless there is at least the possibility of fulfilling them. The basic promise of God, I would say, is the implicit promise already present in the human vocation to personhood and community.

There is, of course, an alternative reading of the situation. Conscience, vocation, inner constraint and the rest may have an illusory character, they may be laying upon us the obligation to what is *impossible*. This is the conclusion reached by those who say that human existence cannot be other than self-frustrating. On this view, ought does not imply can; and this is also to say that 'ought' is meaningless.

On the other hand, when we speak of promise, we cannot mean anything like 'guarantee.' We have seen that a promise is a reciprocal relation, and involves the promisee as well as the promiser. The promise is that the vocation, obligation and so on are possible of fulfilment, not that they will be fulfilled automatically and no matter what human beings may do. This makes it clear that what we are here calling 'promise' is very closely related to what in the first chapter we were calling 'hope.' It is indeed the same phenomenon seen from a different aspect and in another context. It will be remembered that we sharply distinguished hope from any shallow optimism or doctrine of universal progress. Yet we found that hope seems to accompany everything that human beings do. Hope is the faith that what we are doing is—to use again St. Thomas' words—difficult but possible of attainment. God's promise is the other side of human hope, and its ground. What is most difficult is the fundamental task given to every one of us—the task of becoming an authentic human person in relation to other persons. But we hope that the task is not an impossible one, because the promise of the possibility of fulfilment is already given in the vocation to existence.

Here we have been trying to fix the meaning of the expression 'promise of God' in its most general sense, and we have found it in the implicit promise that is given with existence itself. The example from the Old Testament that most clearly corresponds to this fundamental promise of God is the promise given to Eve. In the story, 'she was the mother of all living' (Gen. 3, 20). We may regard her as the primal human existent, coming to that first awareness of the human vocation to be in a world where there is also diminution of being (sin) and loss of being (death). She is called to live and to bring forth living beings and to fulfil the promises of life in an ambiguous world where everything affirmative is threatened. The promise is stronger than the threat and supports the hope of fulfilment. But again there is no optimism in the promise, but rather there is the prospect of conflict, with the eventual attaining of that which is difficult but possible: 'God said to the serpent, "I will put enmity between you and the woman, and between your seed and her seed; he shall bruise your head, and you shall bruise his heel" ' (Gen. 3, 15).

Promises, however, whether they are made by human beings or by God, have usually a much more specific content than that very general and basic promise which, we have claimed, is already given with human existence and finds mythological expression in the so-called *protevangelium*. The question of specificity will, moreover, become important when we ask about the way one establishes whether or not a promise has been fulfilled. So we must look at one of the more specific promises of God in the Old Testament and see what meaning we can attach to that.

We take as an example the promise of God to Abraham. This is in fact quite a specific promise, and there are several items in it. There is the promise of a land or country; of a great nation to be descended from Abraham; of a great name or fame for Abraham as the founder of the nation; and of a 'blessing,' not clearly defined, both for Abraham and, through him, for 'all the families of the earth' (Gen. 12, 1–3). We do not suppose that God literally spoke these words to Abraham. We remember too that the words of the promise are not reported by Abraham himself (if indeed there was an individual called Abraham) but that the promise is given its shape by biblical writers of many centuries later who posited some such event at the beginning of the history of the nation. What I am saying is that the specificity of the promise comes from the human beings who reported it, not directly from God himself. Furthermore, the particular items are reported by writers of long afterwards who, having the benefit of hindsight, were able to state much more clearly the content of the promise than Abraham (assuming that there was an Abraham) could have done at the time of receiving it. And even to these people of long after, the full content of the promise was still not clear—I have referred already to the vagueness of the promised blessing. The original promise of God was something still implicit and not yet put into words—a vocation, an inner sense of constraint. But human beings can only understand and communicate anything of the sort by putting it into language, and as time goes on and the situation unfolds, the verbalizations become fuller and more specific. There is a parallel here between promise and revelation. We do not suppose that revelation was originally given in words, yet from the beginning, from the primordial encounter with God, men have tried to put the revelatory experience into words.

I think we can say the biblical writers, living in the consciousness of Israel's election and vocation, gave a true interpretation of what must have been the experience of the founder of their people, whether Abraham or someone else. But that interpretation is given in the light of the subsequent history, and the experience of the promise on the part of the original hypothetical Abraham would be much simpler and less specific. Indeed, it would probably not be very different from what we have already described when discussing the promise given in Eden. It would be a coming to consciousness of the promise already implicit in human existence itself. I have often been struck by the remarkable resemblance between the beginning of the Abraham stories and what Sartre says about human existence. According to Sartre, the distinctively human existence comes about when man separates himself from the predetermined framework of Nature and decides to be 'for himself.' He rejects any ready-made essence. 'We mean that man first of all exists, encounters himself, surges up in the world—and defines himself afterwards. If man is not definable, it is because to begin with he is nothing. He will not be anything until later, and then he will be what he makes of himself.'[16] Likewise Abraham rejects the pattern of life found in the cities of Mesopotamia —a predetermined pattern founded on the past. He turns to the desert, to the area which is as yet undetermined and unformed—one might almost say the nothing, the meontic area. Before he has gone into that area, he cannot say in advance what he will learn or find there. But his vocation to go there is already a promise. Perhaps there is a minimal content, perhaps even the thought of a land, a people, a blessing as later generations believed. But these are only human verbalizations and interpretations of the primordial divine promise of existence, and they might change with deepening experience. Thus the hypothetical Abraham could hardly have been aware of the universal scope of the blessing which later generations ascribed to him; on the other hand, a time might come when the need for a land or country as an item in the promise came to seem unnecessary.

These remarks have relevance when we ask questions about how one would know whether a promise of God had been fulfilled, or how one could judge whether such a promise had been falsified. Human promises are, generally speaking, sufficiently specific and limited that we can without much difficulty say whether they have been kept or broken or just forgotten. If I promise to meet you at three o'clock, and duly appear at that hour, I have kept the promise. If I promise to pay you five pounds for tidying up my garden but give you only four, I have broken my promise. But no such simple criteria seem to operate when we are thinking of the promises of God. His basic promise is to give us more abundant life. But we cannot specify the conditions of such life in advance. It is only in the unfolding of history and the actual deepening of human life that we can say whether the promise is being fulfilled. This could well mean that it is fulfilled differently from the way we had at one time expected, for our expectation could be framed only in terms of what we had experienced up to that point, whereas the fulfilling of the promise might bring with it something new.

The promise to Abraham was specified in terms of a land, a nation, renown and a blessing, and one could say that all this was fulfilled in the story of Israel's conquest of the promised land and the establishment of the kingdom. But what can be made of the events that came after that? The kingdom was first divided, and in course of time the two smaller kingdoms disappeared. The land was overrun and oppressed by foreigners. The people ceased to be a political entity and was dispersed through the world. The holy city of Jerusalem with its Temple, the visible symbol of all the hopes and aspirations of Israel, was desolated. Was not this outworking of events a plain falsification of the supposed promises of God?

Certainly it was a falsification when the promise is specified in terms of a land, a political entity and a glorious destiny, as measured in conventional terms. It seems likely too that this was a shattering blow to the faith of Israel and that there was a widespread lapse into paganism. But among the exiles were some who were driven by these events to consider the promise anew, and to respecify it. Was God to be understood at a deeper level as not just the God of Israel but the God of all the earth? Did this mean in turn that he was not tied to a particular holy site or to a particular land? Did this mean that his people could be conceived as a community of faith rather than a political entity or earthly kingdom? Again, was their blessing and their fame to lie in their dissemination of the knowledge of God to all nations? Or would there come a time when the scattered tribes would return to the holy city, and when all nations would flow to it?

It is very difficult to know how to answer these questions. Probably only a few people came to think of the destiny of Israel as the bearer of God's word to the nations, and saw in that the deepest fulfilment of the promise. Others cherished the thought of a return. Still others in course of time developed the fantastic visions of apocalyptic, which might seem to be the last desperate attempt to cling to the promise in the face of all the contrary evidence.

Since we are dealing with a matter of faith, not of demonstration, the question whether the promise was falsified or whether it came to be more deeply understood and therefore to be specified anew, cannot be conclusively answered. Indeed, the question is still being debated, though in new circumstances. What are we to say of the sufferings of the Jews in this twentieth century, especially in death camps like Auschwitz? Richard Rubenstein finds these events a falsification of the promise, the end of the road for the eschatological God. 'After the experiences of our times, we can neither affirm the myth of the omnipotent God of history nor can we maintain its corollary, the election of Israel.'[17] Rubenstein sees the re-establishment of the Jewish state in Palestine not just as a return to the land but as a return to the gods of the land, the nature gods of paganism who had been worshipped before there arose the illusion of a Lord of history. But a different construction is put on these events by Abraham Heschel. He acknowledges that 'intimate attachment to the land, waiting for Jewish life in the land of Israel, is part of our integrity.' But he sees the return to Israel not as a denial of the God of promise but as a new evidence: 'What should have been our answer to Auschwitz? We did not blaspheme, we built. Our people did not sally forth in flight from God. On the contrary, at that moment in history we saw the beginning of a new awakening. Is the State of Israel God's humble answer to Auschwitz?' A little further on, he writes: 'And yet, there is no answer to Auschwitz. To try to answer is to commit a supreme blasphemy. Israel enables us to bear the agony of Auschwitz without radical despair, to sense a ray of God's radiance in the jungles of history.'[18] So the hope of Israel persists even in our own time, and though it has been tested to the very limits of endurance, no one could say that it has been falsified as long as there are men and women prepared to accept it and commit themselves to it and find meaning in it in their own times.

But before we conclude this chapter, let us return to another of the promises of the Old Testament (or perhaps we should say, to another aspect of the one promise of God). I mean, the promise of a messiah. No ideal ruler of the house of David appeared to sit on the throne of his fathers and to bring in the reign of justice and peace. No flaming apocalyptic Son of Man descended from the heavens to judge the earth, punish the wicked and reward the righteous. The mainstream of messianic expectation was, if you will, falsified. What came to specify the promise anew were some quite marginal utterances by an unknown prophet of post-exilic times. He had sung of one whose rule would consist in service to the peoples of the earth, and whose service in turn would consist in bringing forth justice through his own suffering (Is. 42, 44, 49, 53). Here was a radical respecification indeed; and it was this respecification that was taken up by Christianity and given a definite content as the continuation and fulfilment of the promise to Israel.

Notes
[1] Mircea Eliade, *Cosmos and History: The Myth of the Eternal Return*, tr. Willard R. Trask (Harper Torchbooks, New York, 1959), p. 89.
[2] Gerhard Von Rad, *Old Testament Theology*, tr. D. M. G. Stalker (Oliver & Boyd, Edinburgh, 1962), vol. I, p. 136.
[3] John Bright in *Peake's Commentary on the Bible*, ed. M. Black and H. H. Rowley (Thomas Nelson, London, 1962), p. 499.
[4] Walther Eichrodt, *Theology of the Old Testament*, tr. J. A. Baker (SCM Press, London, 1961), vol. I, p. 245.
[5] See above, p.13.
[6] See below, p. 47.
[7] R. H. Charles, *Eschatology: The Doctrine of a Future life in Israel, Judaism and Christianity* (Schocken Books, New York, 1963), p. 61.
[8] See above, p. 25.
[9] See above, p. 40.
[10] See below, p. 79.

56 CHRISTIAN HOPE

11 Rudolf Bultmann, History and Eschatology (Edinburgh University Press, 1957), p. 155.
12 Plato, Timaeus, 37.
13 Plato, Republic, 514ff.
14 Alvin Toffler, Future Shock (Bantam Books, New York, 1970), p. 326.
15 Jürgen Moltmann, Theology of Hope: On the Ground and the Implications of a Christian Eschatology, tr. James W. Leitch (Harper & Row, New York, 1967), p. 42.
16 Jean-Paul Sartre in Existentialism from Dostoyevsky to Sartre, ed. Walter Kaufmann (Meridian Books, Cleveland, 1956), p. 290.
17 Richard L. Rubenstein, After Auschwitz: Radical Theology and Contemporary Judaism (Bobbs-Merrill, Indianapolis, 1966), p. 69.
18 Abraham Joshua Heschel, Israel: An Echo of Eternity (Noonday Books, New York, 1967), pp. 44, 112-115.

III
Christ Our Hope

There is perhaps no document of the New Testament that conveys more clearly the sense of living in a new dawn than the Epistle to the Ephesians. It expresses the life of a new community, even of a new humanity. It speaks of the breaking down of divisions and the overcoming of alienations. It comes out of the experience of those who believed themselves to be living through the fulfilment of God's ancient plans and promises, those who 'first hoped in Christ' and those who had been in the state of 'having no hope, and without God,' 'strangers to the covenants of promise' (Eph. 1, 12 and 2, 12). The new community of hope has been described by Henry Chadwick in the following words: 'It is not that by baptism Gentiles are incorporated into Judaism, like synagogue proselytes. Nor does it mean that Christian Jews abandon the promises of God given to their fathers. The Church is God's new creation, and Christians are a "third race" (to use the language of some second-century Christian writers), though not in such a sense as to be discontinuous with the old covenant. Gentile Christendom is universalized Judaism. Both Jew and Gentile, united in Christ through his reconciling death, have access by one Spirit to the Father.'[1]

In the new community, the horizons of the hope that had been born in the experience of Israel were vastly expanded. But equally the hope was deepened and acquired new content. This transformation of hope had come about through Jesus Christ—indeed, he was himself the hope of the new race.

Jesus Christ, according to the belief of the first Christians, had fulfilled the promises and hopes of the old covenant. I have myself written elsewhere that 'if there is any validity at all to the sense of a constraining power which men call "God" and which summoned Abraham from his home and worked on all those who came after, the lines converge unmistakably on Jesus Christ.'[2] Yet it must be acknowledged that this judgment is made only retrospectively and from the standpoint of Christian faith. To be sure, we have noted already that universalizing tendencies were appearing in the latest prophetic sections of the Old Testament, and that there were marginal images of the servant of the Lord that were to become central in Christianity. But much more consideration will have to be given to the question of how Jesus Christ fulfils the hope of Israel, and we shall have to use some such flexible version of the promise–fulfilment schema as was outlined in the last chapter. But flexibility cannot be made an excuse for interpreting a promise in any way that happens to suit us. We must respect the integrity of Israel's hope as it finds expression in Israel's own scriptures, and I think this means that we must respect the integrity also of modern Jewish writers such as Abraham Heschel who claim to see Israel's hope being fulfilled in other ways. Perhaps the promises of God and the religious idea of a 'total hope' are sufficiently comprehensive to embrace both Christian and Jewish expectations.

A whole new content is injected into the idea of hope by the resurrection of Jesus Christ. We have seen that the idea of resurrection had already emerged in Judaism. But hitherto it had been an expectation; resurrection was an event that still lay ahead. But now, according to the Christian proclamation, resurrection has happened. Admittedly, it is the resurrection of one man, Jesus Christ; but he is not considered simply as an individual, but as the firstfruits of a new humanity. Of course, the resurrection of Jesus Christ is one of the most difficult, controversial and vulnerable items in the Christian creed. On the other hand, it is one of the most central, and under-pinned the new community of hope. If Christ is risen from the dead, then the concept of hope has been radically transformed and enriched. On the other hand, if Christ is not risen from the dead, it is hard to disagree with Paul when he tells us that in that case, 'our preaching is in vain and your faith is in vain' (II Cor. 15, 14). So we must study very carefully the meaning and grounds of Christian faith in the resurrection of Christ.

There is still another dimension to the new Christian hope. Christ would come again. Just as he was seen as the fulfilment of the long ages of messianic expectation, so he had become the object of a new expectation. To begin with, his return seems to have been expected very shortly. But as time went on, that return was deferred to some indefinite date in the future. The origins of the belief in the coming again of Jesus Christ are obscure, and some scholars have even argued that it arose from a mistaken interpretation of his teaching. But

however the belief may have originated, it became incorporated into
the scheme of Christian doctrine and stands firmly in the creeds of the
Church: 'He will come again with glory, to judge both the quick and
the dead.' Once again, the fulfilment of one promise and expectation
has led into a new promise and expectation. Perhaps this is a process
to which there will be no end. One could visualize that there might be
a fulfilment so complete that there would be no possibility of any
further hope or promise. This is presumably what St. Thomas had in
mind when he wrote: 'Hope will pass away in heaven, just as faith
will, and so neither of them is to be found in the blessed ... Hope
exists only in those who are still *en route*, whether in this life or in
purgatory.'[3] But it may possibly belong to the very nature of the
relation between the infinite and eternal God and his creatures that
every fruition to which the creatures come is the opening of a new
promise and a more distant horizon. So thought St. Gregory of Nyssa:
'The progression of our desire directed toward God cannot be halted
by any satiety ... The perfect life is one in which no limit is set to
progress in perfection.'[4] If this is so, then whatever may have been
the origin of a belief in the second coming of Christ, it nevertheless
represents a true spiritual insight.

This chapter then will be devoted to exploring the hope that is in
Christ under the three topics just mentioned—*Christ as the fulfilment of
Israel's hope, the resurrection of Christ,* and *the hope of his coming with glory.*

1. *Christ as the Fulfilment of the Hope of Israel*

'For the Son of God, Jesus Christ ... was not Yes and No; but in him,
it is always Yes. For all the promises of God find their Yes in him'
(II Cor. 1, 19–20). In these emphatic words Paul expresses his
conviction that the hope of Israel, inspired by all the promises of God,
had found its fulfilment in Jesus Christ. This is now indeed the
accepted Christian belief, so that when we hear Paul's words today,
they may seem to be stating something obvious. But that is only
because we hear them as Christians whose understanding of these
matters has been formed by nearly two thousand years of tradition.
When Paul first made such a claim for Jesus Christ, his words must
have seemed novel and startling even to those who were disposed to
believe them, while to those not so disposed, they must have seemed
sheer nonsense.

We have ourselves seen enough of the problems and difficulties surrounding the promise–fulfilment schema in biblical theology to acknowledge that the claim that Jesus Christ is the Yes to all the promises of God in the Hebrew scriptures does demand some examination and cannot just be accepted as obvious. After all, it was not obvious to most of Paul's contemporaries among those who were versed in the scriptures, and it never has become acceptable to those who continue in the old covenant. What grounds then do we have for claiming that Christ has fulfilled the hope of Israel? Can we show that the tradition, which now makes such a claim appear obvious to the Christian, is theologically well founded and not merely one that has arisen fortuitously?

Of course, the interpretation of Jesus Christ as the Yes to all the promises of God, as the fulfilment of the hope of Israel, was only possible in retrospect. It is not being suggested that he was explicitly the object of Israel's hopes, or that those who entertained those hopes in pre-Christian times would have recognized Christ as the fulfilment. We have already seen how, as experience grows, an individual or a people, looking back, interprets the hopes and promises of the past in new ways and sees their fulfilment differently. The Old Testament hope and promise, which centred at first on a land, a people, a name, a blessing, and later on a restorer and a return, were not being falsified by the course of events but were being understood in an increasingly profound way. Still, all that was something like a reforming of the hope and promise, and when we move on to Jesus Christ, there is not a reformation but a revolution in the understanding of these matters.

It is worth remembering that the life of Christ himself was understood in retrospect, and that is how it is presented in the gospels. After it was over, but not before, it was seen as the carrying out of a pre-ordained plan of God. It is the end of that life, the passion, death and resurrection, that is presented most fully and vividly in the gospels. What went before is shown as leading up to the end. The ministry is narrated in much more sketchy fashion than the passion. The years of childhood, youth and formation are passed over practically in silence. The birth stories are manifestly legendary, and beyond them the story is extended further back into time by a speculative idea of pre-existence. It is this account of the career of Jesus Christ, itself understood retrospectively, that then attracts to itself the promises of God to Israel and then gives them a new retrospective interpretation. But the new interpretation is so violent that, as already said, it revolutionizes rather than reforms the expectations. For Jesus Christ is no political ruler, no messianic king, no restorer of Israel, no supernatural judge from heaven, but the suffering servant, the most marginal of all the images born of the prophetic imagination. Viewed retrospectively, the passion dominates the foreground. And in the reconstruction of its antecedent events, the passion still dominates, even, let us say, in the legendary stories of his birth. The birth in a cave or a stable is of a piece with the rest. There is a remarkable passage in the writings of philosopher Ernst Bloch, in which he says: 'The stable is true; so mean an origin is not invented for a founder. Myths do not paint misery, and surely not a misery that lasts a lifetime. The stable, the carpenter's son, the fantast among little people, the gallows at the end—this is historical stuff, not the golden tapestry beloved of legend.'[5] These remarks of Bloch may provoke a derisive smile from the New Testament critic. Yet he is right, for even if the stable is legend, one may agree that the stable is true—theologically true, in the first instance, because it has reflected the cross into the very origins of Jesus' life, but even historically true, because in a very profound sense this story is throwing light on the history that had begun in Israel (or further back) and is now approaching its consummation.

I have ventured to speak of 'the history which began in Israel—or even further back.' What is meant by this expression, 'even further back'? It makes allusion to a phrase that we find scattered through the New Testament—'from the foundation of the world' or 'before the foundation of the world.' Christ was 'destined before the foundation of the world,' even if he has only been 'made manifest at the end of the times' (I Pet. 1, 20). He was beloved of the Father 'before the foundation of the world' (John 17, 24). A kingdom has been prepared for his followers 'from the foundation of the world' (Mt. 25, 35). These same disciples were chosen 'in him before the foundation of the world' (Eph. 1, 4). Christ, it was believed, had pre-existed from the beginning. Even before history began to run its course, Christ and his saving work were present in the mind and intention of the Father. Of course, this had only come to be known in retrospect. But now, in the light of Christ's historical appearing, there is seen the 'plan of the mystery hidden for ages in God who created all things' (Eph. 3, 10). The promise of Christ, then, had been there from the beginning. And now that it had been revealed, everything else fell into place—all the intervening promises and covenants, all the specific expectations with which succeeding generations had given them content. These were not contradicted, but they were now seen to be only temporary moments in the unveiling of God's purpose, now fully known in Christ.

Underlying such beliefs is a philosophy of history, according to which concrete historical happenings (or at least some particularly significant happenings) throw light on the meaning of history as a whole. This underlying philosophy seems to be essential to any belief in revelation or in a religious interpretation of reality. Something similar was given classic expression by Hegel when he wrote: 'That the concrete act [of sacrifice] may be possible, the absolute Being must from the start have implicitly sacrificed itself.'[6] It is of the very nature of Spirit to pour itself out in a kind of *kenosis* so as to participate in finite existence. It is worth recalling that in that New Testament *locus classicus* to which kenotic christologies make their appeal, there are in fact two moments of emptying or humiliation: there is the self emptying of the divine Son before the incarnation, and there is the actual historical self humbling of the human Jesus in his obedient acceptance of the cross (Phil. 2, 7, 8). Of course, the eternal self emptying within God is known only through the historical self humbling of Jesus Christ, but if one accepts Jesus Christ as the revelation of God, then one seems bound to accept that Christ and his sacrifice have from eternity been prefigured in the Father or promised by the Father, even if one has to avoid some of the more mythological ideas of pre-existence.

Theologically, our understanding of these questions can be advanced by attending to Karl Barth's teaching about the humanity of God. To talk of the humanity of God was a sufficiently startling departure from Barth's earlier stress on the otherness of God as to call for some explanation on his part. The humanity of God, he tells us, is 'God's relation to and turning towards man; it signifies the God who speaks with man in promise and command.'[7] Humanity has always been enclosed in the very deity of God. 'It is precisely God's *deity* which, rightly understood, includes his *humanity* ... Who God is and what he is in his deity, he proves and reveals not in a vacuum as a divine Being-for-itself, but precisely and authentically in the fact that he exists, speaks and acts as the *partner* of man.'[8] Barth seems to imply that from eternity God has committed himself to man, so that, in a sense, the incarnation is already promised in the creation of man. It is the man, Jesus Christ, who therefore fulfils the promise of God

and who gathers up in himself all previous ways of understanding
God's promises.

But when we speak of Christ's gathering up the earlier interpretations of God's promises, we must not minimize the way in which these
earlier interpretations had to be radically transformed. We have
already used the word 'revolution' in this connection. A land, a
people, a name, a destiny, a judgment of the nations—these items
may all have had their proper place in the process of education in
the ways of God, but now they all seem irrelevant or even trivial as
the promise gets its definitive fulfilment in the suffering servant,
powerless except for the power of love. It meant a revolutionary
change not only in men's understanding of the promise of God, but in
their understanding of God's very nature, for his nature and his
promise cannot be separated. This revolutionary change is finely
expressed by Barth himself, who tells us that if we are in earnest in
taking Jesus Christ as our point of reference, then 'the mystery
reveals to us that for God it is just as natural to be lowly as it is to
be high, to be near as it is to be far, to be little as it is to be great,
to be abroad as it is to be at home.'[9] And here we may link again
with the thought of Ernst Bloch, who, as we have seen, insists on
the truth of the stable as expressing the humility of God's advent.
The good news of Christianity, he believes, is that it abolishes 'everything that smacks of a power deity,' 'every myth or mythical element
of lordship and mastery that reflects power and effects an ideology
of power' as found in the cult of the pre-Christian gods, whether
Baal or Marduk or Ptah or Jupiter—or even perhaps Yahweh in
some ways of thinking of him.[10] Nor can it be denied that the
revolution has sometimes been reversed, and the Christian God too
turned into a national or cultural power symbol, as Barth so
devastatingly showed in his early writings.

The new Christian assessment which took Jesus Christ as its
central clue from which to look back over history even to the hidden
purposes of God himself revolutionized the understanding of the
promises of God and even of the nature of God when it made the
claim that in Christ all these promises have found their Yes. This
was the true transvaluation of values, perhaps the greatest revolution
in values that has ever happened. To be sure, there was continuity
with the tradition—the belief in a God who creates and who in that
very act of creation thereby commits himself and gives a pledge and
a promise, together with the history of the hope and promise through

Abraham and the others—all this was taken over and understood from a Christian perspective. But the content and future of the promise were understood in a radically new manner.

An interesting parallel can be drawn between the revolutionary change in men's understanding of the promises of God that came with Jesus Christ, and the revolutionary changes that sometimes take place in our understanding of particular sciences. Martin Heidegger pointed out many years ago that progress in the sciences consists 'not so much in collecting results and storing them away in manuals' as in revolutionary crises when the basic concepts of the science need to be drastically rethought. 'The real movement of the sciences,' he wrote, 'takes place when their basic concepts undergo a more or less radical revision which is transparent to itself. The level which a science has reached is determined by how far it is capable of a crisis in its basic concepts. In such immanent crises, the very relationship between positive investigative inquiry and those things themselves that are under interrogation comes to a point where it begins to totter.'[11] He then illustrated his point from contemporary developments in mathematics, physics, biology, history and theology. The notion of scientific revolutions has been taken up and elaborated by Thomas Kuhn.[12] His thesis is that normal scientific work goes on within the framework of a generally accepted paradigm or model, which serves to guide investigations. But in course of time, various anomalies appear. To some extent, these can be taken care of by making modifications in the controlling paradigm. But eventually the pressures become so great that the controlling model collapses, and a new paradigm takes its place. This is a 'scientific revolution.' A familiar example would be the change from Ptolemaic to Copernican astronomy. Astronomers kept adding epicycles to the old geocentric model to account for the movements of the heavenly bodies, but at last the whole system had become so complicated that it was falling apart, and the time was ripe for that drastic shift of models which we call the Copernican revolution.

Though the parallel is not exact, one could point to something analogous in the history of the interpretation of the promises of God. In the last chapter,[13] we have indeed seen how the promises kept on being modified and reinterpreted in the history of Israel. In the latest period, the modifications were so extreme (apocalyptic, universalism, even perhaps the suffering servant idea) that there had developed a very untidy state of affairs as compared with the

relatively straightforward promises that were supposed to have been
made to Abraham. But with the coming of Christ and Christianity,
there takes place a shift so drastic that it could justly be compared
to the Copernican revolution in astronomy.

I deliberately say, 'with the coming of Christ and Christianity,'
for it would be hard to disentangle precisely what came from Christ
himself and what from his followers. Did he, for instance, think of
himself as the suffering servant of deutero-Isaiah's prophecy, or was
this model applied to him by the infant Church after his crucifixion
and resurrection? This is an historical question, and any answer to it
will never have more than a degree of probability. But however the
question gets answered, it would not seem to be of any great
theological importance. Jesus Christ, as an individual, merges into
the community which is indeed called his body, just as any individual
merges into the social context without which he could not exist. No
doubt Jesus Christ inaugurated the new understanding of the
promises of God, whether by actual teaching or simply by his career,
but there can be no doubt that the process of revolutionary reinterpretation continued among his disciples.

But is there any evidence for this revolution in theological understanding, and can we know anything about how it proceeded? We
do indeed have some glimpses of it.

David Strauss was already grappling with this problem. He
believed that the process of reinterpreting and transforming the Old
Testament promises occupied the Church for a generation. We
glimpse it, for instance, in the incident of the two disciples on the
way to Emmaus (Lk. 24, 13ff). The prophet, 'mighty in deed and
word,' whom they had followed in the hope that he would redeem
Israel, had been put to death. But now the risen Christ himself comes
to them and shows the necessity of his sufferings: 'And beginning with
Moses and all the prophets, he interpreted to them in all the
scriptures the things concerning himself.' On Strauss's view, this was
part of a revolutionary reinterpretation of the Old Testament on the
part of the Church. Passages which had never before been regarded
as messianic were now attached to Jesus, regardless of the original
intention of their authors. In particular, the novel (or almost wholly
novel) idea of a suffering Messiah was vindicated, and the revolution
completed, so that the claim was made that Jesus had fulfilled all the
promises of God. As Strauss saw it, the work of interpretation worked
in two directions. Unmistakably messianic predictions in the Old

Testament had to be satisfied in the life of Jesus, so that some incidents and reports are to be understood as fabrications designed to make Jesus fit the messianic profile. Such, for instance, would be the report of his birth at Bethlehem, the city of David. On the other hand, events which had undeniably taken place in the life of Jesus, especially the events of his passion, had to be given a justification from the Old Testament. Thus the suffering servant passages became central in the Christian interpretation of Old Testament messianic prophecy. Strauss writes: 'As he who has looked at the sun, long sees its image wherever he may turn his gaze; so the disciples, blinded by their enthusiasm for the new Messiah, saw him on every page of the only book they read, the Old Testament, and in the conviction that Jesus was the Messiah, founded in the genuine feeling that he had satisfied their deepest need—a conviction and a feeling which we still honour—they laid hold on supports that have long been broken and which can no longer be made tenable by the most zealous efforts of an exegesis which is behind the age.'[14]

Strauss is here acknowledging that the story of Jesus is not just a fabrication made to fit messianic expectations but is even more a memory of a real person so impressive that the tradition and its promises came to be read in quite a new way. He does indeed suggest that this was an untenable exegesis, and admittedly if exegesis consists in eliciting the meaning which the authors originally intended, then the messianic interpretations put on the Old Testament by the early generations of Christians were mistaken. But interpretation is surely not restricted to the exegesis of what was in the mind of the author. Interpretation is itself a creative act, and indeed the Old Testament authors had themselves creatively interpreted their own inherited traditions. The reality of Jesus Christ, brought into confrontation with the Old Testament tradition, wrested new interpretations from it, and these interpretations did not falsify it but brought out possible depths of meaning of which the original authors had been unaware. An inspired writing, whether in religion or literature, has precisely this kind of inexhaustibility. The language contains an overplus of meaning, so to speak, beyond what the writer understood and beyond what his interpreters have understood at any given time.

We have tried to understand the way in which the hope of Israel became transformed in a revolutionary manner into a hope centred in Christ, seen as the one in whom all the promises of God found their Yes. We have also seen that this transformation came

about by a legitimate process of creative reinterpretation in the early
years of the Christian Church—a reinterpretation more drastic than
any that had happened before, yet not essentially different from the
many reinterpretations of the promises of God that had taken place
in the history of Israel as the people's experience deepened and new
vantage points were reached for a more comprehensive retrospect of
history. But certainly there is no way one could demonstrate that
Jesus Christ is the fulfilment of the hope of Israel. To claim that he is
such fulfilment remains for us, as for those who first made the claim,
a judgment of faith. But it is not a groundless judgment. We can
understand how it arose, and we can test it by standing at this
vantage point, Jesus Christ, looking back over the history of promise
and even into the mystery of the God who originated the promise,
and judging whether, at the deepest level of interpretation, the lines
do converge on him.

2. *The Resurrection of Jesus Christ*

In discussing the question of how Christ can be seen as the fulfilment
of the hope of Israel, we have deliberately kept the question of his
resurrection in the background. For the main problem which stood in
the way of accepting him as the fulfilment of the messianic promises
was his passion. This is what made him an 'offence' to most of his
contemporaries. But it was precisely his passion which opened the
new and deeper understanding of God as one who stands with his
creatures amid the sins and sufferings of the world, and is not therefore a distant celestial monarch, untouched by the travail of creation.
This in itself is a ground of hope. But it would fall short of that
total hope which seems to be the peculiarly religious hope. There
would be the question whether this God who comes among men in
humility and who stands with them in the world has also the power
to overcome the evils of the world and to bring his creatures into a
new situation. It is at this point then that one must go on to ask
about the resurrection of Jesus Christ as a further essential component
of the hope that centres in him.

It must be already clear to us that the resurrection cannot be
understood in any way that would simply cancel out or reverse the
passion. If the suffering Messiah is in his suffering the true fulfilment
of the promises of God, then it must be through the travail of that
suffering that resurrection is to be attained. Again, if through the

revelation in Christ we have got away from the old monarchical conceptions of God, we must continue to see God in the new way, that is to say, to learn about God through Christ. There is always the temptation to go back to the pre-Christian *deus ex machina* whose chief characteristic is power and who exists to put things right when they have gone wrong. But if the God whom we meet in Christ is a God whose only power is love, then the resurrection does not annul the passion. Rather we must think that God absorbs it into himself, and that his own life of love is stronger than the sins of men, and opens a new way forward.

Karl Barth remarks in one place that Good Friday is the day of the Father, Easter the day of the Son, and Whitsunday the day of the Holy Spirit.[15] We would not question the allocation of Whitsunday to the Spirit, but is Barth right in his allocation of Good Friday and Easter Day? Should we not think of Good Friday as the day of the Son, the day of his sacrifice for mankind? And then we would think of Easter as the day of the Father, when he raises his Son from the dead. But then we would be in very grave danger of making the mistakes mentioned in the last paragraph—the mistakes of cancelling out the passion and turning the Father into a convenient *deus ex machina*. So deeper reflection leads us to believe that Barth is at least partly correct in his ordering of the days. Good Friday is a day of darkness, and not just the darkness that is said to have overshadowed the land during the time of the crucifixion, but the metaphysical darkness surrounding the hiddenness of God. 'He made darkness his secret place, his pavilion round about him with dark water, and thick clouds to cover him' (Ps. 18, 12). Even the Son experienced this darkness—or perhaps especially he: 'My God, my God, why hast thou forsaken me?' (Mk. 15, 34). When we claim that we learn about God from Jesus Christ or that he is the revelation of the Father, we do not mean that the whole inexhaustible mystery of God is laid bare—this would be impossible. We do mean however that in Christ we have our best clue to the mystery of the Father and that there is nothing in the Father that contradicts what we have learned in Christ. Easter is the extension and deepening of the hope already encountered in the self-giving death of Christ—the hope that love is stronger than death and will eventually triumph. Easter is the day of the Son not in the sense that through an almighty intervention of the Father the darkness of Good Friday has been scattered and its agony abolished, but that through that agony the Son has emerged as the living centre of a new life and new hope for all mankind.

So we confront the mystery of the resurrection. The idea of resurrection, as we have seen, was not new. It had emerged in the history of Judaism and had become more and more accepted. But it was no more than an idea, a hope. Now, it was claimed, resurrection had actually happened. Jesus Christ, on whom the lines of promise had converged, was risen from the dead. This unique claim lies at the very centre of Christian hope. But it is also one of the most fragile items in Christian faith, reminding us again that hope itself is fragile and vulnerable. How can anyone believe in a resurrection? Surely it is no more than an illusion, born somehow in the brains of the disappointed followers of Christ. Not only sophisticated moderns find the report of the resurrection incredible. It has always been so. When Paul preached at Athens, he seems to have received an attentive hearing until he mentioned the resurrection—then his audience laughed (Acts 17, 32). Yet odd and improbable as the report of Jesus' resurrection must seem, it is the keystone in the structure of Christian hope. It is the foundation of the new promise which the Church ascribed to Christ: 'Lo, I am with you always, to the close of the age' (Mt. 28, 20). And we have already agreed with Paul that if Christ is not risen, then the Christian proclamation is vain and Christian faith is vain. The resurrection of Jesus Christ is the *articulus stantis et cadentis ecclesiae* in the strictest sense, the central article of belief by which Christianity stands or falls. Philosophers sometimes challenge the Christian theologian to say what would falsify Christian faith, for if it is impossible to specify what would falsify it (so they say), then it must be something so vague and lacking in content as to be not worth affirming. Perhaps the answer to this demand that the theologian should specify a state of affairs that would falsify Christian faith has already been given by Paul: 'If Christ has not been raised, then our preaching is in vain and your faith is in vain.' Here we seem to get a straightforward answer to the question of what would falsify Christian faith.

Yet it is not so straightforward as it seems at first glance. For what, after all, is meant by the resurrection of Jesus Christ? It is very clear from Paul's own writings that he did not understand by the resurrection of Christ simply that the dead body had been resuscitated. When there is talk of the resurrection of Christ, we come into an area where the language has to be sorted out very carefully, for the historical and the mythical, the literal and the metaphorical, the subjective and the objective, are all blended together. Perhaps only a language with this kind of complexity is adequate for talking of an event so extraordinary, but it is a language full of traps for the unwary.

Where do we begin an attempt to understand and evaluate the belief that Jesus Christ has risen from the dead? Clearly, we have two possibilities. We may begin from present experience. If the promise that Christ will be present with his people until the close of the age is true, then the experience of his living presence ought to be available in the Church today. Since the time of Schleiermacher, theology has set a very high value on present experience as a theological datum, and no doubt many contemporary theologians would agree with Schleiermacher that it is on the basis of present experience that Christians affirm Christ to be alive in their midst, and so give credence to the doctrine of his resurrection.[16] We shall come back later to this question of present experience. But there is the other possibility that one begins from the scriptural reports. There we have the earliest testimony to the resurrection of Christ, and while it may be the case that we would never believe these reports unless we had some present experience that seemed to confirm them, nevertheless it is in the New Testament that we find attested the origins both of the belief and the experience, and so we shall begin from the New Testament witnesses.

The New Testament evidence itself falls into two distinct strands. There are stories about the discovery of an empty tomb, and stories about appearances of the risen Lord to his disciples. The details of the empty tomb story vary from gospel to gospel as regards the precise time in the morning at which the tomb was visited, the number and names of the women disciples who went there and exactly what they saw and heard; but there is agreement that women, going to anoint the body of Jesus in the tomb, found not a body but an empty sepulchre. Likewise there are variations in the reports of appearances, as to whom they were made, under what circumstances and in what localities; but again there is agreement that some of the disciples, both individually and in groups, experienced visions and locutions which they interpreted as meaning that Christ was still alive in their midst.

Scholars differ as to the relative importance which they attach to the two strands of tradition. According to R. Bultmann, the story of the empty tomb is 'a quite secondary formation,' and 'the purpose of the story is without doubt to prove the reality of the resurrection of Jesus by the empty tomb.'[17] So on his view, belief in the resurrection arose from the disciples' experiences of the appearances of the risen Christ, and the story of the empty tomb is a later legendary objectification. He points out that Paul's mention of the resurrection is our earliest written testimony to the event, and that while Paul mentions a series of appearances, he apparently knows nothing of an empty tomb. But perhaps this last point about the priority of Paul has less force now that John Robinson has shown that the conventional dating of the New Testament documents rests on more flimsy foundations than has often been realized, and that the gospel records may well be much closer to the events they record than has usually been supposed.[18]

A very different view from Bultmann's is held by G. Vermes, who believes that it was indeed the empty tomb (however one is going to explain it) that originated the belief in the resurrection of Jesus. He writes: 'In the end, when every argument has been considered and weighed, the only conclusion acceptable to the historian must be that the opinions of the orthodox, the liberal sympathizer and the critical agnostic alike—and even perhaps of the disciples themselves—are simply interpretations of the one disconcerting fact: namely, that the women who set out to pay their last respects to Jesus found, to their consternation, not a body but an empty tomb.'[19] This statement from a reputable historian who has no special theological axe to grind must at least make us hesitate before accepting Bultmann's contention that the empty tomb story is a later legendary embellishment of the belief in the resurrection.

On the other hand, if we suppose that belief in the resurrection did have its origin in the discovery of an empty tomb and even if investigation led us to believe in the probability that this tomb was in fact empty, could anything of importance for Christian faith or theology be established on this basis? I do not think that it could—certainly not on the basis of the empty tomb alone. There could be many explanations of an empty tomb. The women may have gone to the wrong tomb; or the disciples may have secretly removed the body, as has often been alleged from an early date onward; or there may have been some other 'natural' explanation. Let me acknowledge at once, however, that the explanations I have mentioned are not very convincing. An important point to remember too is that it seems highly unlikely that the disciples were expecting any resurrection. No doubt they believed, like the Pharisees, that there would be a resurrection of the dead at the end of the age, but this is quite a different belief from belief in the resurrection of a particular person, Jesus of Nazareth. The report of the resurrection of Jesus took the disciples by surprise, and this seems to rule out the explanation either that they contrived the empty tomb or that they jumped to the conclusion that Jesus must have risen from the dead because his tomb was found empty. On the contrary, Mary Magdalen is said in one account to have offered a natural explanation for the empty tomb—'They have taken the Lord out of the tomb, and we do not know where they have laid him' (Jn. 20, 2)—while in another account it is said that the disciples dismissed the women's story as 'an idle tale' (Lk. 24, 11).

However, the conscientious historian, seeking to explain the events of history by other events within the same stream, would have to exhaust every possible 'natural' explanation that he could think of. For instance, even if he thought poorly of the explanations of error or fraud mentioned in the last paragraph, he might suggest others that imply nothing so odd as the raising of the dead. He might think it possible that Jesus had not been quite dead when taken down from the cross, though he appeared to be dead, and that in the cool of the sepulchre he had revived and gone away. This too may be improbable, but the point I want to make is that even if one is bound to consider the empty tomb tradition with more seriousness than some New Testament scholars have accorded to it, very little of a theological nature could be built upon it. There is no straightforward route from the empirical fact of an empty tomb to the raising of the dead by God. And here we may notice a point of some importance that confirms what I have been saying. In the New Testament, the empty tomb tradition does not appear as the sole evidence that led the disciples to believe in the resurrection of Jesus, but is supported by stories of post-resurrection appearances.[20] By contrast, Paul mentions as evidence the appearances without mention of the empty tomb. I would then say that the reports of the appearances constitute the most important New Testament evidence for the resurrection of Jesus, and it is to them that we must devote most attention.

We are using the neutral expression, 'appearances.' Was what appeared or was seen, the actual physical body of Jesus, restored to life? Were the appearances subjective to the experience of those who received them, or were they objective phenomena? No clear or consistent answers to these questions can be found in the New

Testament, though we may note that the risen Jesus appeared only
to believers, and this would seem to point away from any understanding of the resurrection as an objective happening. It is true that
Luke and John seem to stress the materiality of the Lord's resurrection body. The disciples are invited to touch him to assure themselves that he is bodily present with them (Lk. 24, 39 and Jn. 20, 27).
But even in these gospels the risen Lord sometimes behaves in ways
which imply that his is not an ordinary physical body, and in all the
New Testament writers the risen Lord is not just the dead Jesus
revived, but Jesus gone on to a new mode of existence.

It is not possible for us to consider all the reported appearances of
the risen Lord, and I shall concentrate on what Paul has to say on the
subject. Paul's account of the appearances is our oldest written
testimony to the resurrection, and claims to be based on a still older
tradition which the apostle had received. That does take us back
pretty close to the events, since Paul was writing not much more
than twenty years after the crucifixion of Jesus. He mentions
appearances to the principal disciples (I Cor. 15, 5–7), some of the
appearances having been to individuals, some to groups of apostles,
and one 'to more than five hundred brethren at one time, most of
whom are still alive, though some have fallen asleep.' There is cited
also the appearance of the risen Lord to Paul himself, and it is
interesting that this appearance, of which we have accounts elsewhere in the New Testament, is clearly reckoned by the apostle to be
of the same order as the appearances granted to Peter, James and
other of the original disciples. Finally, having testified to the
appearances of the risen Christ, Paul goes on to discourse at length
on the nature of resurrection (I Cor. 15, 12–57). This theological
exposition of his not only helps us to know what he himself meant
by his claim that Christ has been raised from the dead but lays the
foundation for further theological reflection on the theme.

But does the appeal to reports of appearances really carry us any
further than the reports of the empty tomb? If the latter are
susceptible of various natural explanations which may be more or less
convincing, is not the same true about the appearances? Here, let
us admit, the explanations would be somewhat more sophisticated,
but they would be none the less natural. They would be explanations
in terms of psychology, the mechanism of visions and locutions and
hallucinations, the possibility that deeply cherished expectations
might lead to the illusion that they had been fulfilled, and so on.

Also, since mass or group hallucinations sometimes occur, the fact (or reported fact) that Christ appeared to the twelve or even to five hundred disciples at once would not carry much more weight than reports of his appearances to individuals.

There is, however, one awkward fact that stands in the way of any easy acceptance of a purely psychological explanation, and that is the fact (on which there is widespread agreement among New Testament scholars) that the disciples were not expecting a resurrection. We took note of this point in connection with the story of the empty tomb— the women did not expect to find it empty. But the point is even more significant when we are considering the appearances, for people only 'see' things which are not there when they are expecting to see them. But if, as seems likely, the death of Jesus had disappointed his followers of the hope that he was to be the one who would redeem Israel, there was no predisposition of mind that would account for the occurrence of hallucinatory visions. The exception, of course, is Paul himself. As Strauss had already noted, this is one difference between the appearance to Paul and the earlier appearances to the original disciples: Paul was already aware of the belief that Jesus had risen, while the original disciples knew only that he had died.[21]

But although the antecedent circumstances of Paul's experience were different, we come back to the point that he understood the experience itself to be of the same order as the experiences of Peter and the others whom he mentions. This must make us wonder how seriously we are to take the sensuous or physical details of these experiences, as does also Paul's subsequent reflections on the nature of resurrection. If we forget for the moment the vivid details of Paul's conversion given in Acts, and attend to his own account, he says simply that 'God was pleased to reveal his Son to me' (Gal. 1, 16). This revelation may well have been accompanied by a sensation of light and by hearing in his mind words of Jesus, but what is essential to it is a revelatory encounter with God in Christ. We can say then that the experience of Paul is continuous not only with the experiences of those to whom the Lord had earlier appeared, but with all subsequent meetings or encounters with Christ in the history of the Church—meetings which may occasionally in a few exceptional individuals have taken the intense form of visions, but which in the great majority of cases would be simply a sense of the presence of Christ, or of God in Christ, sometimes more and sometimes less distinct. There is a deliberate vagueness in my choice of words, 'the presence of Christ, or of God in Christ.' This reflects an imprecision in the New Testament itself, where the risen Christ and the Holy Spirit of God are not clearly distinguished. The risen Christ is experienced always as the Christ of God. We are at the furthest remove from some kind of spiritualist *séance*, where contact is made with the soul of a deceased person. The presence of Christ is experienced not as contact with a departed individual, Jesus of Nazareth, but as communion with the Christ of God, living in God and mediating God. Perhaps it is for this reason that it is more correct to say (as the New Testament writers frequently do) that Christ was raised by God or that God raised him up, rather than that he rose from the dead, as if this were something that he had done in and by himself, and as if he continued to exist as an individual entity rather than within the life of God.

The foregoing considerations seem to be directing us to some such conclusion as follows. Belief in the resurrection, so far as it is dependent on reports of appearances of the risen Christ, does not rely on the visions, locutions or other sensuous details associated with such reports. The details are in any case confused and inconsistent. The steady datum which underlies all the stories of visions, and which connects them with later experiences of the risen Christ, including our contemporary experiences, is the sense of the presence of God in Christ and of Christ in God, or, to put it in another way, the sense of the presence of a God in whom Christ is alive and whose Spirit is the Spirit of Christ.

But this means in turn that the appeal is finally to religious experience. In some individuals, that experience does take the extraordinary form of visions and the like. This may have been the case with Mary Magdalene, Peter, Paul and other early Christian disciples, though we have to allow for the probability (fairly clear in the case of Paul) that their experiences have been dramatized and pictorialized in the telling. This may also have been the case with some exceptional later Christians. But the appeal is to the broad stream of continuous Christian experience, which claims to know the presence of the living God, and in knowing God knows Christ, in knowing Christ knows God.

So the question about the possibly illusory 'appearances' is not so simple as asking whether psychology can give a 'natural' explanation of visions and the like. It turns into the much deeper one of the validity of religious experience as a whole, and especially man's sense of a presence which he calls God. Psychology and sociology can no doubt help to account for the particular forms which this sense assumes in different cultures, but it would be a reckless assertion, going far beyond what can be reasonably based on psychology or sociology, that would claim that religious experiences of God are nothing but subjective happenings in the mind. As John Bowker has ironically remarked, 'The possibility cannot be excluded that God is the origin of the sense of God.'[22]

I am saying then that in the present experience of the Church, in its common life, in its prayer and worship, in its proclaiming and hearing of the word, above all, in its celebration of the eucharist, there is an awareness of the presence of God; and not just of any God, but the God who is in Christ, so that in knowing the living presence of the Father, we know also the living presence of the Son who is alive in the Father and we realize the truth of his promise to be with us to the end of the age. I am saying too that this present experience is, at its deepest level and leaving aside sensuous experiences which might accompany it in the case of exceptionally constituted individuals, continuous with the experience of the risen Lord granted to the first disciples.

Now this assertion of a continuity of experience is of great importance. It was Ernst Troeltsch who enunciated the principle of analogy as fundamental for the work of the historian.[23] The principle states that the report of an event will be more or less probable to the extent that we can point to analogous events in present experience. Thus the report of a resurrection would be very difficult to accept unless we could point to some present experience. In the present case, reports that Christ after his death had appeared to and been present to his disciples would be enormously strengthened in their probability if we today can point to moments in our experience when we have known the presence of Christ-in-God.

It seems to me a great weakness in the recent attempts by Moltmann and Pannenberg to rehabilitate belief in the resurrection of Jesus Christ that neither of these theologians has paid sufficient heed to the principle of analogy—in fact, they have very little concern for present experience at all, and tend to leap straight from the past to the future. Moltmann holds that the resurrection of Christ was a unique event of the past, and that there are no present analogues; but he claims that the analogy will be provided in the future, when there takes place the general resurrection of the dead.[24]

Pannenberg too excludes any present experience from consideration. But whereas Moltmann pays at least lip service to the principle of analogy, Pannenberg rejects it. It introduces 'a constriction of history based on a biased and anthropocentric world-view.'[25] The resurrection of Jesus Christ is an event of the past to be established by historical investigation of the past, and Pannenberg believes that resurrection is the best explanation of the reported events. But both Moltmann and Pannenberg are in serious trouble. Although they inveigh against 'positivist' historians, they both want to claim that Christ's resurrection was in some sense an objective historical event. Yet they also insist that resurrection was not a crudely literal revival of a dead body, and that the term is metaphorical. What meaning then could we attach to it, unless we had some present experience to shed light on it—and this is what they both deny. It is hard not to conclude that what Van Harvey once said about Karl Barth is even more applicable to Moltmann and Pannenberg: they claim all the advantages of history, but will assume none of its risks.[26]

Moltmann and Pannenberg are both in more or less violent reaction against Bultmann and the latter's attempt to demythologize the resurrection of Christ. But, with some qualifications, I think it may be claimed that it is Bultmann who affords a better entry into the understanding of resurrection. Bultmann's approach is the reverse of Pannenberg's, that is to say, it is present experience, not past event, that is the clue to understanding resurrection. Thus Bultmann says: 'Christ meets us in the preaching as one crucified and risen. He meets us in the word of preaching and nowhere else. The Easter faith is just this—faith in the word of preaching.'[27] I would not myself want to lay all this stress on preaching, because for those of us who espouse the sacramental tradition, the eucharist is the meeting place par excellence with the crucified and risen Lord. But that is not an important point in the present argument. The central issue on which Bultmann is right is that in the Christian life as we know it now, there is a living encounter with Christ which is also an encounter with God.

But there is another important strand in Bultmann's way of understanding resurrection. It is not just that in the experience of word and sacrament we are addressed by the living word of God-in-Christ and know his presence, it is that in that experience the Christian himself knows something of the inward meaning of resurrection. Here Bultmann bases himself on Paul's teaching that the life of the Christian is a sharing or participation in the life, death and resurrection of Christ, an identification with him beginning in the sacrament of baptism and continuing through life. 'So you also must consider yourselves dead to sin and alive to God in Christ Jesus' (Rom. 6, 11). Thus Bultmann can say that 'in everyday life Christians participate not only in the death of Christ but also in his resurrection.'[28] To have faith in the resurrection of Christ, on this view, is not primarily assenting to the belief that at some date in the past Christ rose from the dead, but rather the present experience through Christ of a life that has been renewed and revivified, a life so closely merged into the life of God that the Christian knows it as eternal life. This is 'knowing the power of his resurrection' (Phil. 3, 10), and surely this is the most profound and significant way in which we can know what resurrection is. This is the analogy (missing in Moltmann and Pannenberg) which for the first time opens an understanding of the mystery of resurrection.

It is on this basis too that we can believe also in the resurrection of Christ as past event. At first sight, it might seem that in Bultmann's interpretation the past has been wholly swallowed up in the present and even that the resurrection of Christ has been turned into an entirely subjective experience of Christians. It can hardly be denied that Bultmann himself seems to lean in these directions. It could be argued that for him, Christ rises only in the kerygma or perhaps in the new community of the Church. Resurrection, on such a view, would be something that occurred not in and for Christ himself, but in and for the redeemed community that sprang up from his blood. But whatever Bultmann's own view may have been, I do not think that such a 'reductionist' interpretation of the resurrection is either theologically adequate or historically plausible.

It is true that Christ lives on in the Church and its proclamation, just as it is true that everyone, to some extent, can be said to live on for some time in his friends and loved ones, for persons are open to each other and each enters into the other. But this does not exhaust what we mean by the resurrection of Christ. We have to remind ourselves that the disciples were not looking for a resurrection, but were on the contrary depressed and defeated after the crucifixion. They did not generate their own resurrection life out of their own resources or out of nostalgic memories of a dead leader. Their sense of resurrection depended on their belief that Jesus had already risen in himself. This would have been the case even if they had been expecting him to rise from the dead. The Church and the kerygma only arose because—so the disciples certainly believed—Jesus had arisen and was alive for ever, and their experiences attested this. In some cases these experiences may have taken dramatic visionary form, but most no doubt had their experiences of the risen Lord through the more ordinary but no less persuasive media of the prayers, the fellowship, the breaking of bread.

Can we say anything further about this resurrection of Jesus himself, a firm belief in which seems to be the only plausible explanation for the rise and enthusiasm of the early Christian community? Whatever we may say must be to some extent speculative. The gospels themselves do not describe the resurrection—it is the event posited between the story of Christ's death and the stories of the empty tomb and his reappearances. Paul does provide a substantial piece of theological reflection on the nature of resurrection, but even so it is guarded and is perhaps as important for excluding misunderstandings of resurrection as it is for affirmative teaching on the subject. Thus it is made clear that resurrection is not the bringing to life again of the physical or natural body: 'it is sown a physical body, it is raised a spiritual body. If there is a physical body, there is also a spiritual body' (I Cor. 15, 44). The conception of a spiritual body is a difficult one, but what seems to be implied is that the 'body' is to be understood not crudely as the organic structure of flesh and blood and bone and so on, but as the manner of personal insertion into a world, whether a world of things or persons. A spiritual body would seem to mean a new mode of existence in which the person is incorporated into the life of God. It is clear too that Paul thinks of this as the potential destiny for all human beings, though Jesus Christ is the first to have attained to it.

This line of thought connects with some of the matters on which we have touched earlier. Christ is the fulfilment of the promises of God, he is the one in whom the destiny that God appointed for human beings has been fulfilled. That destiny was to become like God himself and to enter into the closest communion with God. At an early stage in this book[29] it was said that the human being lives in continuous self-transcendence and that in hope he projects himself even beyond death. If Jesus Christ is the fulfilment of the humanity which in others is incomplete or disfigured, must we not suppose that this is also the meaning of his resurrection? This man Jesus has transcended to a perfect union with the Father (he has 'ascended into heaven,' in the traditional language), so that he now lives as one sharing in the eternal life of God. When we talk of Jesus Christ fulfilling the possibilities of human existence, then we do not mean that he has fulfilled *all* possibilities—here we may recall the point that a finite human existence cannot be fulfilled by becoming a 'bloated' existence, but only by dying to some of its possibilities. Jesus, we may say, dying to all else, fulfilled the most essential godlike possibilities for man—love, freedom, integrity, creativity.

We could express similar ideas by recalling that the evolutionary process on this planet has proceeded not only by steady advances but also by leaps which could not be foreseen but become visible only after they have happened. Such, for instance, was the transition from non-living to living, and then the transition from merely living to personal. The resurrection of Jesus Christ may be compared to a leap of that sort. There is, of course, an important difference. The earlier emergences occurred through the unconscious operation of natural laws, but once human beings with their power of self-determination had appeared, any new advance could take place only through the free co-operation of the human being with God, as indeed was the case with Christ.

This discussion of the resurrection of Christ and of the hope based upon it may now be summed up in three points. 1. Jesus himself, having fulfilled the essential possibilities of human existence and attained to union with the Father, lives in God on a new level of existence, which we call the resurrection life. 2. In a variety of ways Christians participate in the dying and rising of Christ, and it is through their present experience of life in the body of Christ that they already have some understanding of the meaning of resurrection and eternal life. 3. The final author of all this is God himself, so that resurrection can be understood also as a fundamental aspect of God's activity in the world, namely, his opening up of new possibilities for life and still more abundant life.

3. *The Hope of His Coming Again*

We have seen how each hope leads into a new one, and each new hope is more comprehensive than the one that went before. The hope of Israel went through many stages of deepening and development, and found its fulfilment (so Christians believe) in Jesus Christ. With his resurrection was born a new hope, the hope of the eventual triumph of his Spirit over all the evil and negative forces in the world. The faith and hope of the Church is that 'he will come again with glory.'

What do we mean by this expression, 'with glory'? It cannot be understood in a way that would detract from what has already taken place in Christ's first advent. It is not as if there is something deficient in Christ that is to be made up at some future time. Still less could it mean that the suffering Messiah is to be replaced by some triumphant superman. What we have already learned of the humanity of God rules that out, and we can agree with Barth when he writes somewhat angrily: 'If Jesus Christ is the word of truth, then Nietzsche's statement that man must be overcome is an impudent lie.'[30] The human itself has enough of transcendence and openness to be the vehicle for the divine. In resurrection and even in deification, it remains human. 'Human nature, at the contact of God, does not disappear,' writes John Meyendorff; 'on the contrary, it becomes fully human.'[31] Christ's coming again with glory, then, may be a fuller hope, but it is not a different hope from the one that has been there since men began to hope—the hope for the fulfilment of the promise already implicit in the creation of man.

Talk of Christ's second coming is so laden with mythological connotations that perhaps we should begin by stripping some of these away. There are several saying of Jesus in the gospels in which he speaks of the coming of the Son of Man, apparently understood as a heavenly judge who would come in the near future with glory upon the clouds to bring the age to a close (Mt. 25, 31, etc.) It came to be believed that in these sayings Jesus was speaking of himself and of his imminent return, but it seems possible or even probable that originally Jesus was thinking of an apocalyptic figure with whom he did not identify himself. The identification may first of all have taken place in the minds of the disciples. Paul, for instance, in his early letters seems to expect that Jesus would return from the skies within the lifetime of his own generation to institute his reign (I Thess. 4, 16). So it may have been a misunderstanding of the words of Jesus or a mistaken application of them that first led to the expectation of his return. In fact, it did not take place, and the whole question had to be rethought. But it is quite in line with what we have already learned of the dynamics of hope and promise that the first ways of understanding them are only first approximations, and have to be clarified and refined in the light of further experience. Once the disciples had come to believe that Jesus was the Christ, then there could be no expectation of another different from Jesus, and what he himself may have said concerning an expected Son of Man had to be applied to himself; and once it became apparent that the return was not going to be so speedy as had at first been supposed, then the vivid mythology of the heavenly figure descending from the sky was replaced by more sober reflection on what the end of Christian redemption might be.

In some cases we can actually trace these transitions in the New Testament. For instance, Luke says: 'Every one who acknowledges me before men, the Son of Man also will acknowledge before the angels of God' (Lk. 12, 8), and it is at least an open question whether Jesus and the Son of Man are the same; but in Matthew the identification is definitely made, for he says: 'Every one who acknowledges me before men, I also will acknowledge before my Father who is in heaven' (Mt. 10, 32). In II Peter we get a glimpse of the murmurings that arose as time passed and the end of the age still did not come: 'Where is the promise of his coming? For ever since the fathers fell asleep, all things have continued as they were from the beginning of creation' (II Pet. 3, 4). In John's gospel we read that the believer has already 'passed from death to life' (Jn. 5, 24) and that 'now is the judgment of this world' (Jn. 12, 31), and with such expressions we seem to have moved from future expectations to the view that the end is already taking place. Assuming that John's gospel comes from near the end of the first century, the expectation of a speedy return of Christ from the skies had faded, and is replaced by a kind of realized eschatology. This eschatology is also spiritualized, and it may be that in this gospel the Holy Spirit, whom Jesus had promised to send 'in his name' and who would be with the disciples 'for ever' (Jn. 14, 15–17 and 25ff.) is to be understood as none other than the returned Christ. A tendency toward a realized eschatology is to be seen too in the mature thought of St. Paul, when the expectation expressed in the early letters had not been fulfilled.

So we may have a sequence somewhat as follows: 1. Jesus expects the speedy advent of the apocalyptic 'Son of Man' and understands him as someone other than himself; 2. The disciples identify Jesus with the Son of Man and expect his imminent return from heaven; 3. When this does not happen, the entire expectation is, if one may use the expression anachronistically, 'demythologized,' at least, to a considerable degree, though the expectation of a return in the indefinite future lingers on.

Here once more it has to be asked whether this process of modification of the original hope is not just a refusal to admit that the hope had been falsified by the course of events—and the question is given extra force by the fact that the modification seems in part to have been due to plain misunderstanding. But I think that the considerations which we had in view when we reflected on the modification of the hope of Israel can be paralleled in the case of the Christian hope. The essence of that hope was the disciples' conviction that something new and lifegiving had appeared in Jesus Christ, and when the first mythological formulations of the hope turned out to be inadequate, new and more satisfactory formulations were sought, for the essential insight remained that Jesus Christ is a hope-creating reality. At the same time, it has to be acknowledged that the New Testament does not reconcile the future expectation of Christ's return with the so-called 'realized' eschatology of John and Paul. The tension has remained in all subsequent Christian theology, as we shall see. Realized eschatology does not entirely swallow up future expectation, and when it seems to do so (as was already the case even in John) there soon comes about a reaction, and the future expectation is again declared to be an inalienable part of the Christian tradition. Most recently, this tension is exhibited in the divergent interpretations of eschatology to be found in Bultmann on the one hand and Moltmann and Pannenberg on the other.

But even where future expectations remain, the second coming of Christ has come more and more to be understood symbolically as the triumph of his cause than as his personal return. Thus the second coming merges into other eschatological ideas, especially the kingdom of heaven and the resurrection of the dead. These ideas too are susceptible of various interpretations. The kingdom is in one sense a present reality, already inaugurated by Jesus Christ. But who would claim that it had been realized, either in the Church or in society at large? Perhaps a few churchmen in times of triumphalism have thought that the kingdom was realized in the Church, and a few sectarians may have thought that it was realized in some utopian community, but sober theology seems bound to admit that the fullness of the kingdom is not yet, so that the kingdom retains a future dimension. The case is similar with the resurrection of the dead. No doubt Christians have in a sense already passed from death to life, and I have emphasized the importance of a present experience of resurrection. But this is far short of the original hope of a renewal that would redress the wrongs and injustices of history. Even if we were to believe that at some future time a perfectly loving society were to come into existence, or that some radical transformation of the human race were to take place, this could not be judged a fulfilment of that total religious hope for the whole creation, if it left untouched the fate of those who had unjustly suffered in all the ages. After all, we have seen that belief in resurrection was closely associated in its origins with the demand for justice.

Thus, although the New Testament finds in Jesus Christ a new hope which enlarges and enriches the hope that had been inherited from Israel, there are unclear features in this hope, especially in its language about Christ's coming again, the kingdom of God and the resurrection of the dead. The New Testament leaves us with un-answered or only partially answered questions about hope, and we have to pursue these into the continuing history of hope in Christian theology.

Notes
[1] Henry Chadwick, 'Ephesians' in *Peake's Commentary on the Bible*, ed. M. Black and H. H. Rowley (Nelson, London, 1962), p. 980.
[2] J. Macquarrie, *The Faith of the People of God* (S.C.M. Press, London, 1972), p. 55.
[3] Thomas Aquinas, op. cit., 2a2ae, q. 18, a. 2 and 3.
[4] St. Gregory of Nyssa, *Vita Moysi*, II, 239 and 315.
[5] Ernst Bloch, *Man on His Own*, tr. E. B. Ashton (Herder & Herder, New York, 1970), p. 180. The chapter quoted is excerpted from *Das Prinzip Hoffnung*.
[6] G. W. F. Hegel, *The Phenomenology of Mind*, tr. J. B. Baillie (Allen & Unwin, London, 1910), p. 722.
[7] Barth, *The Humanity of God*, tr. J. N. Thomas and T. Wieser (Collins, Fontana Library, London, 1967), p. 33.
[8] Barth, op. cit., p. 42.
[9] Barth, *Church Dogmatics*, IV/1, tr. G. W. Bromiley (T. & T. Clark, Edinburgh, 1956), p. 192.
[10] Bloch, op. cit., p. 114.
[11] Martin Heidegger, *Being and Time*, tr. J. Macquarrie and E. S. Robinson (S.C.M. Press, London, 1962), p. 29.
[12] Thomas Kuhn, *The Structure of Scientific Revolutions* (University of Chicago Press, Chicago, 1962).
[13] See above, p. 54.
[14] D. F. Strauss, *The Life of Jesus Critically Examined*, tr. George Eliot (Swan Sonnenschein, London, 1906), p. 582.
[15] Barth, *Church Dogmatics*, I/1, tr. G. T. Thompson (T. & T. Clark, Edinburgh, 1936), p. 382.
[16] Friedrich Schleiermacher, *The Christian Faith*, tr. H. R. Mackintosh and J. S. Stewart (T. & T. Clark, Edinburgh, 1928), p. 428.
[17] Bultmann, *The History of the Synoptic Tradition*, tr. John Marsh (Harper & Row, New York, 1963), p. 284ff.

[18] J. A. T. Robinson, *Redating the New Testament* (S.C.M. Press, London, 1976).

[19] Geza Vermes, *Jesus the Jew* (Collins, London, 1973), p. 41.

[20] This statement would not be true of St. Mark's gospel, if it ended at 16, 8; though it would still be true that confirmatory appearances are promised in 16, 7.

[21] Strauss, op. cit., p. 741.

[22] John Bowker, *The Sense of God* (Clarendon Press, Oxford, 1973), p. 16.

[23] E. Troeltsch, 'Ueber historische und dogmatische Methode in der Theologie,' *Gesammelte Schriften* (J.C.B. Mohr, Tuebingen, 1922), Band II, p. 729ff.

[24] Jürgen Moltmann, *Theology of Hope*, tr. J. W. Leitch (S.C.M. Press, London, 1967), p. 180.

[25] Wolfhardt Pannenberg, *Basic Questions in Theology*, tr. G. H. Kehm (S.C.M. Press, London, 1970), vol. I, p. 45.

[26] Van A. Harvey, *The Historian and the Believer* (S.C.M. Press, London, 1967), p. 158.

[27] Bultmann, 'New Testament and Mythology' in *Kerygma and Myth*, ed. H. W. Bartsch, tr. R. H. Fuller (S.P.C.K., London, 1957), p. 41.

[28] Bultmann, op. cit., p. 40.

[29] See above, p. 22.

[30] Barth, *The Humanity of God*, p. 49.

[31] John Meyendorff, *Christ in Eastern Christian Thought* (Corpus Books, Washington, 1969), p. 64.

IV
Hope in Christian Theology

We have seen how the New Testament itself contains a diversity of eschatological teachings and that there remained unresolved problems about what Christians were expecting. It was left for subsequent generations of Christians to think out in greater detail the nature of the Christian hope, but the different understandings already present in the New Testament have tended to reappear in new forms. In this chapter we shall consider some of the more important expressions of Christian hope in the history of theology, bringing the story right down to the debates that are still going on in the twentieth century.

1. A Typology of Interpretations

It may be useful to begin by setting out in a baldly schematic fashion some of the oppositions that go back to the New Testament (and even, in some measure, to the Old), and that have continued to set up tensions in subsequent interpretations of Christian hope.

1. There is the contrast between individual and social conceptions of the eschatological hope. Although the individual's hope for ultimate salvation came later than a collective hope, it has gradually tended to become the dominant form of religious hope. The contrast may be extended further to include not only a social hope but a cosmic hope, that is to say, hope for a new heaven and a new earth and an entirely renewed natural order. This is the grandest of all eschatological visions, and perhaps more than any other would deserve to be called a 'total hope'.

2. There is the further contrast between this-worldly and other-worldly expectations. Again, even if the this-worldly expectation came first, it is the other-worldly expectation that has tended to be dominant in the history of theology. But in our present secularized culture, there has been a move toward reversing the traditional dominance of the other-worldly.

3. A further opposition is that between evolutionary and revolutionary understandings of Christian hope. The first visualizes the

coming of the kingdom by a slow process of growth and might claim some support in those gospel parables which compare the kingdom to a seed which grows into a great tree or to the leaven which works through a lump of dough (Mt. 13, 31–33)—though some New Testament scholars would contest such an interpretation. The second visualizes the coming of the kingdom as the contradiction and overthrow of the existing order. Practical consequences follow from these differences of theology. Upholders of the first view are more likely to stress the need for human effort and cooperation in building the Kingdom, while the second view may encourage the belief that we can only wait for the crisis and the divine inauguration of the kingdom. Again, adherents of the first view are likely to be more friendly toward the existing order in the belief that it is a stage toward the kingdom and may be already exhibiting signs of the kingdom, whereas the second view may encourage hostility to the existing order as something that is already perishing and must be abolished in order that the new may come.

4. Another strongly experienced tension is that between those who appeal to the present and those who look only to the future. The first group believes that the end has already come (realized eschatology) or, if that seems too brazenly optimistic, that at least the kingdom is already in process of being realized (inaugurated eschatology). The other group believes that the end still lies ahead (future eschatology) and in this respect stays closer to the original Christian expectations. Still, it should be remembered that even if the original expectation looked for a future event, this did not exclude 'signs of the times' (Mt. 16, 3) which were already present for those who could interpret them and which testified to the reality of the inbreaking kingdom. Even if new hopes were emerging, the hope and expectation of Israel had been fulfilled. So the contrast between realized and future eschatology is never quite absolute.

It is clear that the options presented by these contrasts can be combined in a great many different ways, so that there have been in fact many interpretations of the Christian hope and many Christian eschatologies. One could set out the options schematically as follows:

A1 (individual)	or B1 (social, cosmic)
A2 (this-worldly)	or B2 (other-worldly)
A3 (evolutionary)	or B3 (revolutionary)
A4 (realized)	or B4 (future)

Theoretically, one could construct sixteen basic types of eschatology out of this table. However, some of the combinations that are possible are inherently implausible. Would anyone in his senses combine, for instance, B1 and A4, and claim that the reign of God is already present in its fullness and that human society and, indeed, the whole cosmos, has already been transfigured? The plain facts of injustice and suffering throughout the creation rule out any such interpretation. But perhaps when people begin speculating on eschatology, they tend to take leave of their senses. Even in New Testament times, it was necessary to give warning against those who held 'that the resurrection is past already' (II Tim. 2, 18), while in the modern world Emmanuel Swedenborg believed that the last judgment took place in the eighteenth century during his own lifetime, and that the New Jerusalem was founded at that time. We do not, however, intend to take note of all the bizarre developments of eschatology and apocalyptic in the Church's history.

It may also be noted that some combinations seem more 'natural' than others. Thus A1 usually goes with B2, that is to say, an individual expectation is usually also an other-worldly one. But this is not always the case, for in Bultmann's thought an individualistic interpretation of eschatology is combined with a this-worldly realization of the end. Again, while B2 and B4 tend to go together (future expectation with other-worldliness), the hope is sometimes for a this-worldly utopia, and this has been characteristic of some of the most recent theologies of hope.

We cannot spell out all the possible combinations, or the variety of modified and intermediate types that are possible. Some of them have been instantiated in the history of theology while others have not. But a survey of some of the more influential forms will be very helpful to us, and as we see their strengths and weaknesses, we shall be better able to judge what place there is for Christian hope today, and what form it might take.

2. *Some Highlights in the History of Christian Hope*

We may begin by considering what might be regarded as the conventional form of Christian hope. By this I mean the hope entertained by most Christian believers, and supported by the common teaching of the Church. This form of Christian hope emerged quite early, almost as soon as the more full-blooded hopes of the New Testament writers had begun to fade, and, with various modifications and refinements, has remained the standard form of hope among Christians down to the present time.

It would be fair to characterize this hope as both individualist and other-worldly. Perhaps when the Christian community was a tiny minority in the midst of a pagan and often hostile society, it was impossible for hope to take any other form. How could there be any hope for the world as a whole, seeing it had rejected Christ and persecuted his followers? And how could there be any hope for fulfilment within such a world, even though one might now have some foretaste of it, especially in the sacraments of baptism and the eucharist?

Although the hope remained vaguely future, the temporal element in it had been greatly dimmed down. No doubt at some indefinite time in the future there would be a general resurrection, judgment and so on, but heaven was now understood in a timeless, Platonist way, as a parallel but invisible realm existing alongside this world below. So when Christians died, their hope was that their souls would go at once to heaven. John Kelly mentions that even by the end of the first century, St. Clement of Rome believed that Peter and Paul had gone straight to heaven, where they found already gathered a company of saints and martyrs.[1] Two theological consequences would seem to follow from such teaching. One is a doctrine of the immortality of the soul, as against the biblical belief in the resurrection of the body, for how otherwise could the faithful exist in heaven between the time of their deaths and the final resurrection? The other is belief in some immediate judgment of a person at the time of his death in advance of the final judgment, either admitting him to heaven or consigning him to purgatory or hell. The effect of such developments was to deprive the original eschatological expectations of most of their power. An event that had been relegated to a distant future and in any case made superfluous by what was to happen at death, could not create the sense of urgency and energy that the expectation of the end had evoked in the first disciples, not could it be understood as a judgment on the prevailing order, for this was no longer understood as perishing but as likely to last for a long time. These points hold even more strongly after the Constantinian settlement and throughout the era of Christendom, for now the Church was at home in society and any revolutionary sense of eschatology had disappeared.

One may also note the intellectual confusions which accompanied the rise of the conventional understanding of the Christian hope. No doubt these confusions were in part due to the mixing of Hebrew and Greek ideas. Immortality of the soul gets confused with resurrection of the body, a temporal frame of reference has a timeless one superimposed on it, while all the events of the end in the future have to be reduplicated at the death of each individual. Attempts by theologians even down to modern times to sort out all the elements in this conventional understanding of the Christian hope remind one of the endless modifications and refinements that were made to the Ptolemaic system of astronomy until finally it was abandoned for the vastly simpler Copernican scheme. Something like a Copernican revolution seems to be demanded in Christian eschatology, and in fact some modern theologians have attempted it. But we shall come to them later.

It may be thought that I have done less than justice to what I have called the conventional eschatology, since I have presented it in a general way without having regard to the refinements made by specific theologians. It would therefore be fair to consider one classic statement which is essentially a modification of the conventional view but which maximizes its strengths and goes a considerable way toward overcoming its weaknesses. I refer to St. Augustine, whose *City of God* is commonly regarded as the first great attempt to construct a philosophy of history.

I say that Augustine's view is essentially a modification of the conventional view because it shares the basic characteristics that we attributed to the conventional position. Thus Augustine is individualistic in his eschatology; he is resolutely opposed to universalism and teaches a doctrine of predestination, according to which a certain number of the elect will be saved. He is also other-worldly; the background of his thinking is Platonism and the ultimate reality is beyond time and history, in which we can have at most prefigurings.

But the genius of Augustine is that he is willing to incorporate into his thinking something of the truth that lies in the opposite which he has rejected. In other words, there is a dialectic at work, giving his thought a richness and comprehensiveness which the more pedestrian versions of conventional eschatology lack.

Thus, the individualism of his predestination theory is countered by what is the most striking and original feature of his teaching, the doctrine of the two cities. The cities are social or political entities—ultimately, metaphysical entities. As social and political entities, the city of God and the earthly city are locked together in conflict within the world and within history. In a general way, the city of God is represented in history by the catholic Church, the earthly city by the state or civil power. Augustine is therefore sufficiently aware of the ambiguities of history to make possible that prophetic judgment and social criticism which is inherent in the original Christian eschatology but tends to drop out of the conventional version. One recalls his famous question: 'Without justice, what are kingdoms but great robberies?' It is in this connection that Augustine tells the story of a pirate who, having been seized by Alexander the Great and asked what he meant by taking possession of the sea, replied: 'What do you mean by seizing the whole earth? Because I do it with a petty ship, I am called a robber, but you, who do it with a great fleet, are called an emperor.'[2] Of course, as I have said, the two cities are ultimately metaphysical entities and cannot be simply identified with historical institutions. Finally, indeed, only the heavenly city of God has reality, and it lies beyond history. Yet in his dialectical manner, Augustine seems also to be acknowledging that the way to it lies through history.

A different type of eschatological doctrine and one closer to the original expectations is found in such writers as St. Irenaeus and Origen. In different ways, both of these fathers have a vision of the end that is neither individualistic nor entirely otherworldly.

Irenaeus' distinctive contribution is his idea of recapitulation (*anacephalaeosis*), derived ultimately from St. Paul. John Kelly explains the idea 'as implying that the Redeemer gathers together, includes or comprises the whole of reality in himself, the human race being included.'[3] Furthermore, Christ's reign is visualized as an earthly millennium. Irenaeus quotes from Isaiah and other prophets passages predicting a golden age, and urges that they be taken literally. 'If, however, any shall endeavour to allegorize (prophecies) of this kind, they shall not be found consistent with themselves in all points ... But in the times of the kingdom, the earth has been called again by Christ (to its pristine condition), and Jerusalem rebuilt after the pattern of the Jerusalem above.'[4] Though the expression 'after the pattern of the Jerusalem above' seems to indicate that the final reality is an unseen and eternal one, nevertheless the way to it lies through an earthly millennium in history, so that the end that is held up to us is one that is comprehensive, this-worldly and situated in the future.

Origen also teaches a comprehensive hope, though with some differences. He visualizes a universal restoration or restitution (*apocatastasis*). In it even God's enemies will be reconciled to him. Like Irenaeus, Origen finds precedent for his teaching in Paul. 'We think,' he writes, 'that indeed the goodness of God through his Christ may recall all his creatures to one end, even his enemies being conquered and subdued,'[5] and he cites in support Paul's words: 'For Christ must reign until he has put all enemies under his feet' (I Cor. 15, 25). Of course, Origen was strongly imbued with Platonism, and the final end is an intellectual contemplation of God.

It may be accounted a weakness in both Irenaeus and Origen that they seem to have understood the end as simply a restoration of the beginning, though surely one would have to say that the intervening history and, especially, from a Christian point of view, the incarnation and the saving work of Christ, had vastly enriched the potentialities of the end, over against the beginning. Something like a cyclic view of time still lingers in Irenaeus and Origen with history seen as first a falling away and then a return to the eternally perfect ideal. The very language of *apocatastasis* seems to imply something of the sort, since this was the term used for the return of the heavenly bodies to the positions which they had formerly occupied. Still, both of these fathers were preserving essential elements in Christian eschatological teaching—elements which unfortunately tended to fade as the conventional way of understanding the Christian hope became more and more dominant. Especially important was their great vision of the whole cosmos being summed up or perfected in Christ, and this vision can be rescued from cyclic associations and seen as the emergence of the new and the unprecedented, as has in fact happened in the thinking of such theologians of our own century as Lionel Thornton and Pierre Teilhard de Chardin.

The realism of Irenaeus and Origen was lost as the conventional eschatology became more and more influential, especially from Augustine onward. But the more radical element in the Christian expectation was so native to it that it could not quite disappear, and in fact has burst out from time to time in the subsequent history of the Church. But it was now driven into fringe groups and sects, and so it lacked that broad universalism and catholicity that it had had in the earlier times. The expectation remained social but was confined to utopian groups.

An important figure in this line of development was Joachim of Fiore, who flourished in the second half of the twelfth century and was involved in the monastic revival then going on. He tells us that while studying the Revelation of St. John the Divine, 'suddenly the eyes of my spirit were enlightened, and the fulfilment of this book and the harmony between the Old and the New Testaments was revealed to me.' What was revealed to him was the three ages of history. The first age, prepared by Adam and Abraham and initiated by Moses, was the age that revealed 'God the Father in his glory.' The second age, announced by David and others, was ushered in by John the Baptist and 'made known the Son to the Christian people.' The third age, which was still to come but had already been heralded by such monastic figures as Antony, Benedict and Bernard, would 'belong to the Holy Spirit who, during this age, will be shown in his glory, even as the Father was in the first and the Son in the second.' Furthermore, basing his calculation on the fact that St. Matthew's gospel recounts forty-two generations from Adam to Christ, Joachim reckoned that he was already in the fortieth generation of the second age, and that the new age of the Spirit was therefore due to commence in the year 1260. The new age would bring radical change. Just as the age of the Son had abolished the law and the old Israel, so the age of the Spirit would in turn abolish the Church with its priesthood and sacraments and bring in the free spontaneous life of the Spirit. This millennial age, moreover, he understood as this-worldly, and it was to have its political and social consequences in the abolition of feudalism with all its inequalities.[6]

Joachim's teachings were very influential with the radical reformer, Thomas Müntzer. As against Luther, he claimed that the inner light of the Holy Spirit rather than the Bible must be the Christian's guide. His politics were as radical as his theology, and while Luther cultivated the princes, Müntzer supported the peasants in their revolutionary struggle, and is still honoured by Marxists as an early prophet of the classless society. Similar teachings were found among other fringe groups of the Reformation, such as the anabaptists who established a kind of commune in the city of Munster. According to Rosemary Ruether, these anabaptists 'recovered the primitive apocalyptic view of the Church as a transcendental community that leaps ahead of the present world in anticipation of the future age.'[7] England too had its radical millennial sects, which interpreted the Christian hope in this-worldly and political terms. A good illustration is afforded by the Fifth Monarchy Men, active in the time of Cromwell. Their reading of biblical prophecy convinced them that to the four great empires of Assyria, Persia, Greece and Rome, there was now destined to succeed the monarchy of Christ and his saints on earth.

But these apocalyptic sects proved to be transient. As we come to the Enlightenment, eschatology receives a new interpretation. I made the distinction earlier between evolutionary and revolutionary inter-pretations of the Christian hope. The sects had opted for the revolutionary interpretation, but in the Enlightenment it was the evolutionary view that dominated. The traditional eschatology seemed like a remnant of mythology, and its ideas were increasingly intellectualized and secularized. It is very interesting to note that Lessing was acquainted with Joachim's work and believed that his doctrine of three world-ages was 'not just an empty whim.' Lessing himself took over the scheme of the three ages, but he made the last one not the age of the Holy Spirit but the age of reason and edu-cation![8]

Kant's handling of these themes is typical of his time. All the apocalyptic ideas, he tells us, 'can take on, before reason, their right symbolic meaning.' On his view, the coming of the kingdom is to be understood as the gradual transition from ecclesiastical religion to a purely moral religion, to a divine ethical state here on earth. He too preserves the threefold scheme, for religion moves through three stages—the Jewish faith, the Christian faith in its ecclesiastical form, and the purely rational religion that is coming to be. When it does finally establish itself, 'the very form of a church is dissolved, the viceroy [Christ] becomes at one with man who is raised up to his level as a citizen of heaven, and so God is all in all.'[9] One can recognize in this at least a pale reflection of the cosmic consummation en-visioned by the early Fathers and of the age of the Spirit dreamed of by the sectaries. But it has all become highly rational and abstract, and all the urgency and revolutionary sting has gone. It should perhaps be added that Kant, unlike some of his contemporaries and followers, was too realistic in his estimate of the evil in human life to embrace the myth of progress.[10]

Kant, 'the philosopher of Protestantism,' became influential in turn for the liberal theologians of the nineteenth century. In Ritschl's theology, the kingdom of God has quite a central place, and is understood as a this-worldly moral ideal to be gradually realized. He states: 'The Christian idea of the kingdom of God denotes the association of mankind—an association both extensively and intensively the most comprehensive possible—through the reciprocal moral action of its members.'[11] The kingdom of God is not to be identified with the state, though the state is a means to the kingdom. But the kingdom is nevertheless this-worldly. When Jesus said that his kingdom is not of this world, he meant, according to Ritschl, only that it is not a kingdom based on the claims and counter-claims of legal right.[12] Ritschl's ethical gradualist version of eschatology found disciples not only in Europe but in the United States, where it became one strand in the social gospel. Richard Niebuhr has traced the complex course of the idea of the kingdom of God in America, from the early Puritan settlers down to the secularized version in modern liberal theology. It was he who characterized this theology in famous but scathing words: 'A God without wrath brought men without sin into a kingdom without judgment through the ministrations of a Christ without a cross.'[13] This sentence forcefully signalizes the extent of the departure from biblical eschatology.

I have written elsewhere of the difference between liberal theology and radical theology.[14] Both oppose orthodoxy, but in quite different ways; liberalism opposes orthodoxy by accommodating to the cultural and intellectual climate, radicalism by breaking with the prevailing culture, both religiously and socially. The difference is seen most clearly in the liberal and radical interpretations of eschatology. It must be counted one of the tragedies of church history that the liberal theology came to be so dominant in the nineteenth century that it virtually eliminated the apocalyptic notes of judgment and renewal, and watered down the whole eschatological thrust of Christianity. It is well known that when the Church fails to teach some Christian doctrine adequately, that doctrine may reappear in isolation, in a distorted and exaggerated form. This is the phenomenon of heresy. The revolutionary apocalyptic elements in the Christian hope, driven out of the Church, reappeared in secular guise in Marxism.

It may seem strange to make such an assertion, when we recall that right at the beginning of this book I quoted Marx's criticisms of the religious hope. It is true that Marx was critical of every other-worldly expression of hope, since he believed that such hope is alienating.

But we have seen in the meantime that the Christian hope has also its this-worldly significance and that in the thinking of apocalyptic sects it took on a political and revolutionary thrust. The Revelation of St. John can be seen on the one hand as a vision of heaven, bringing a possibly illusory comfort to the victims of oppression; but it can also be seen as a shattering indictment of the established powers of the Roman Empire. This was well understood by Engels in an essay on *The Book of Revelation* published in 1883. He claims that instead of being the darkest book in the New Testament, Revelation is 'the simplest and clearest.' It shows us a picture of the Christian community around the years 68 or 69, and makes it clear that this community was a revolutionary movement made by the masses and opposed to the ruling system. Into the details of Engels' exegesis we need not go, though they make it clear that he had studied the matter rather carefully. But his conclusion is that 'the book is worth more than all the rest of the New Testament put together.'[15] One would not expect Christian scholars to agree with this conclusion, but I quote it to show how the apocalyptic idea was being incorporated into Marxism at a time when Christian theologians had discarded it.

Of course, Marx's apocalypse ran into the same troubles as the expectations of the early Christians, that is to say, things just did not turn out the way that had been predicted. Marx believed that capitalist industrialist society was almost ripe for revolution. In the most advanced industrialized countries, he believed, the workers would become increasingly impoverished and wealth would be more and more concentrated in the hands of a few, until the crash came; and then the whole technological apparatus that had been built up would be available for a new utopian egalitarian society. But things turned out quite differently. In the advanced capitalist countries, the workers became increasingly affluent, and no revolution took place. Marxism was able to establish itself only in backward countries— Russia and eastern Europe, then China and various scattered countries through the undeveloped world. Moreover, the technological apparatus inherited from industrialism was proving itself highly ambiguous, so that neo-Marxists like Herbert Marcuse have been forced to declare that whether in a capitalist or a socialist society, 'technology is not neutral—the technological society is a system of domination.'[16]

It is in the face of this falsification of the original expectations that Rosemary Reuther perceptively comments: 'Thus, as in Christian history, Marxism begins with the announcement of the apocalyptic day of wrath and the speedy advent of the kingdom of God, but ends in the indefinite prolonging of the era of the Church, which can justify all persecution and suppression of liberty in the name of that final liberation which never comes but to which it is the exclusive gateway.'[17] This reminds us too that a gospel of the future can be just as alienating as a gospel of the other world.

Admittedly, neo-Marxists like Marcuse and Bloch talk now of the need for changing human nature as well as social and political structures. But these humane and humanist Marxists are men who have broken with the system and are as much 'heretics' from the orthodox Marxist point of view as were the various apocalyptic sects in Christian history. Still, the new interest in the moral nature of man and the problem of his 'transcendence' lead the discussion once again in the direction of theology. Traditional Marxism is bankrupt of ideas in the face of what is really a spiritual problem, and it is now a question whether Christianity can reunite to itself that eschatological inspiration which was allowed to drain away in the eighteenth and nineteenth centuries.

3. *Twentieth Century Eschatologies*

Actually, a renewed grappling with eschatology has been a very noticeable feature of theology in the twentieth century. It must frankly be confessed that theologians have often given the impression that they just do not know what to do with the eschatological and apocalyptic elements in the Christian tradition, but they have been made very much aware of them. No common mind has been reached, but even today, as we draw toward the close of this century, the eschatological themes that burst on to the theological scene at the end of last century are still very much at the centre of discussion.

The new interest in eschatology began with Johannes Weiss— ironically, a son-in-law of the great Ritschl. Weiss's New Testament studies had led him to the belief that the Ritschlian idea of the Kingdom of God as an ethically ordered society to be gradually realized on earth is a post-Enlightenment idea which has virtually nothing to do with Jesus' understanding of the kingdom. The latter cannot be separated from the apocalyptic expectations prevailing in Jesus' time, and the Ritschlian 'interpretation of the kingdom of

God as an inner-worldly ethical ideal is a vestige of the Kantian idea and does not hold up before a more precise historical investigation.'[18] Rudolf Bultmann has recorded for us his memory of the embarrassment which Weiss's finding caused to the Ritschlian theological establishment: 'When I began to study theology, theologians as well as laymen were excited and frightened by the theories of Johannes Weiss. I remember that Julius Kaftan, my teacher in dogmatics at Berlin, said, "If Johannes Weiss is right and the conception of the kingdom of God is an eschatological one, then it is impossible to make use of this conception in dogmatics." '[19] Weiss had exposed a radical discontinuity between the findings of New Testament historical research and the teachings of systematic theology. But he himself did not follow through on this, and seemed content to let the discontinuity stand, however unsatisfactory this might be. He cheerfully accepted that 'the real difference between our modern Protestant world-view and that of primitive Christianity is that we do not share the eschatological attitude.' We neither believe that the world is passing away nor (even less!) do we pray for its passing. 'We pass our lives in the joyful confidence that *this* world will more and more become the showplace of the people of God.'[20] Moreover, Weiss believed that some of Jesus' most important ethical teaching was non-eschatological in character.

Next came Albert Schweitzer. He acknowledged the value of Weiss's book—'one of the most important works in historical theology . . . it closes one epoch and begins another'[21]—but believed that Weiss had not gone far enough, and that *the whole of Jesus' teaching and ministry* must be understood in a thoroughly eschatological way. A great cultural gulf lies between the ideas of Jesus and his immediate disciples on the one hand and ourselves in the twentieth century on the other. In words that have become famous, Schweitzer declares that Jesus 'will be to our time a stranger and an enigma.'[22] What then can Jesus or the New Testament have to do with us today? At this point I think Schweitzer too sidesteps the issue which he has himself raised. He tries to abstract from the teaching of Jesus an ethic and a religion of love that will be capable of finding expression in the many different world-views that have succeeded the apocalyptic outlook of Jesus himself, but he remains as far as ever from any rehabilitation of eschatology or any attempt to reintegrate the bolder forms of the Christian hope into a modern theology.

Weiss and Schweitzer then did little more than set up the problem

for the theologians who were to come after them. It is to such thinkers
as Barth, Bultmann, Moltmann and Pannenberg that we must turn
for serious attempts to reconstruct a Christian theology that would be
modern and yet would do justice to the eschatological character of the
sources . All four of the theologians mentioned have been discussed at
one point or another earlier in this book, but it will be useful to bring
them together at this stage so that we can see the points of agreement
and disagreement among them and ask ourselves whether out of these
agreements and disagreements we can find a way forward toward a
more adequate theological statement of the Christian hope in our
time.

I believe that the early Barth deserves to be considered as the most
radical Christian theologian of the twentieth century. Of course, he
was writing in a time which must have seemed apocalyptic to those
who were living through it—the aftermath of World War I when
Europe had been shaken to its foundations and the old order had
been cast down. Whereas the liberal theologians, including Weiss and
Schweitzer, had been uncomfortable with the strangeness of New
Testament eschatology, it was precisely the strangeness and otherness
of the biblical revelation that Barth emphasized. Since the Enlightenment, liberal theologians had been trying to show the continuity of
Christian faith and modern culture. Barth accused them of having
domesticated Christianity, thereby depriving it of its offence and its
power. To him the word of God was discontinuous with every human
word and achievement. It was a word of crisis or judgment, breaking
into the human situation in sheer otherness. This, he believed, is
authentic Christianity, and Christ cannot be rightly experienced as
any other than a stranger whose ways are not our ways and whose
thoughts are not our thoughts. He could write: 'If Christianity be not
altogether thorough-going eschatology, there remains in it no
relationship whatsoever with Christ.'[23]

In Barth's eschatology, it would be fair to say, judgment figured
more prominently than hope. Certainly there was nothing senti-
mental about it and it was conjoined with a down-to-earth social
critique. But although Barth never quite lost his early radicalism, he
did come to modify his views. The stress on the otherness of God was
muted to allow a place for the humanity of God, and the strident
eschatological notes of his early writings are scarcely heard in his
dogmatic system. Looking back thirty years later, he acknowledges
that there was a onesidedness in his early teaching, but claims that it

was justified in the circumstances in which he wrote.[24]

Bultmann too accepted the eschatological character of the New Testament. He was just as dissatisfied as Barth with the way in which the nineteenth century liberals had quietly suppressed the more awkward features of the New Testament. 'Harnack,' he complained, 'reduces the kerygma to a few basic principles of religion and ethics. Unfortunately this means that the kerygma has ceased to be kerygma; it is no longer the proclamation of the decisive act of God in Christ. For the liberals, the great truths of religion are timeless and eternal . . . but the New Testament speaks of an *event* through which God has wrought man's redemption.'[25] But Bultmann's way of responding to this situation was very different from Barth's. While accepting that eschatology and apocalyptic are utterly pervasive of the New Testament, Bultmann also teaches that these are mythological elements that have become incredible to modern minds. But they are not just to be eliminated or ignored, in the manner of the liberals. They are to be translated in such a way that the event character of the kerygma and the urgency of the eschatological perspective are preserved, while the unacceptable mythological elements are removed. This, of course, he sought to achieve by existential interpretation. Existential truths are not timeless generalizations, but concrete expressions of self-understanding that have to be appropriated and applied in particular situations. If the word 'eschatological' is most commonly taken to refer to events that come last in the temporal series, Bultmann understands it rather in the sense of events that are indeed temporal but possess 'ultimacy' or 'finality' in the sense of 'decisiveness.' Bultmann's 'eschatological moment' is not the last moment of time (which he would regard as a mythological and untenable idea) but rather something like Kierkegaard's 'moment,' that is to say, the moment of ultimate decision before God. The eschatological ideas of living in the face of the end, judgment, resurrection and eternal life are related by Bultmann to the life of the Christian believer who, as he lives in the face of his own death, experiences renewal and new life through faith in Christ. Admittedly, all this makes sense of the eschatological imagery, and also preserves something of the urgency which eschatology must have carried for those who believed that the time is very short. It may be noted that, like Barth, Bultmann seems to think of the *eschaton* much more in terms of judgment and demand than of hope, and it seems questionable whether anywhere in his writings he gives clear expression to a hope beyond death. Indeed, one might say that Bultmann's treatment of eschatology is the most thorough-going example of a realized eschatology. The last things seem to be brought wholly into the present. But he claims that in doing this, he is simply carrying through a tendency that first appears in the New Testament itself, where Paul and John are already 'demythologizing' the apocalyptic expectations of Jesus and the original disciples. John in particular, it is claimed, 'demythologized the eschatology in a radical manner' so that for him 'the resurrection of Jesus, Pentecost and the *parousia* of Jesus are one and the same event, and those who believe already have eternal life.'[26]

But the last word has not been left to Bultmann. A new phase has opened in the twentieth century revival of eschatology, and the leaders of this new phase have gone further in the rehabilitation of the New Testament preoccupation with the last things than any of their predecessors. I refer especially to Moltmann and Pannenberg. In spite of their differences, we can take them together at this point, for they are much closer to each other than either of them is to Bultmann, and indeed the kind of theology which they represent offers the main alternative to demythologizing, at least, as far as eschatology and the Christian hope are concerned. For Moltmann and Pannenberg, the eschatological ideas of the New Testament are not to be set aside as mythical trappings peculiar to the first century, from which some kerygma is to be disengaged. Rather, these eschatological and apocalyptic ideas constitute the very essence of Christianity. Jesus' resurrection from the dead is no mythological way of expressing the significance of the cross, but an historical event. 'Whether or not Jesus was raised from the dead,' writes Pannenberg, 'is a historical question in so far as it is an inquiry into what did or did not happen at a certain time ... All the talk about Jesus' presence in the congregation is already based on the conviction that he was once resurrected from the dead and not on immediate encounter with the risen Jesus.'[27] Moltmann likewise declares: 'Christianity stands or falls with the reality of the raising of Jesus from the dead by God.'[28] Both theologians object also to the attempt to draw eschatology into present experience, and insist on its future reference. Like Irenaeus and Origen, they look for a consummation, which they call the resurrection of the dead and tend to see in universalist terms. The resurrection of Jesus is the anticipation and guarantee of the final resurrection. The future expectation inherent in the theologies of

Moltmann and Pannenberg helps to give them their strongly affirmative character and justifies Moltmann's expression, 'theology of hope.'

The conflicts between Bultmann on the one hand and Moltmann and Pannenberg on the other are reminiscent of the oppositions which I tabulated at the beginning of this chapter. It will be useful now to draw up a kind of balance sheet as between Bultmann and the theologians of hope, and see if we can discern on which side the weight of truth lies.

On resurrection, I think Bultmann has the advantage that he has been able to relate this idea to something within our present experience. It is not just a speculative or mythical notion, drawn from reports of the past or expectations of the future. Both Moltmann and Pannenberg reject Bultmann's interpretation of resurrection, but they also reject any crudely literal meaning for it. It must be accounted one of the most serious weaknesses of their position that they are unable to attach any clear meaning to 'resurrection,' though this is one of the key terms in their theologies. On the other hand, I do think they have an advantage over Bultmann in positing a resurrection of Jesus that is not just to be identified with the rise of the kerygma or of the Christian community. The conflict here can perhaps be traced to a deeper level. There is a clash between different philosophies of history. Bultmann works with a concept of scientific history (in which there is no place for resurrection as an 'act of God') and with a concept of existential history (in which resurrection can appear as the possibility of renewed existence). Moltmann and Pannenberg are both critical of what they call 'positivist' history and claim that what Bultmann would regard as 'scientific' history has too narrowly positivist presuppositions and ought to be more open to the possibility of unparalleled events, such as resurrection (though once again one would have to ask exactly what they have in mind). But they have certainly not worked out an adequate philosophy of history, and the position is further complicated because both of these theologians are influenced by understandings of history that go back to Bloch, Marx and eventually Hegel.

On the question of the future reference of eschatology, one might think that some advantage belongs to Bultmann's elimination of future expectations and his bringing of the ideas of judgment, eternal life and such like into the present, for it is certainly hard for us to believe in any end or consummation of history in terms of our modern conceptions of the universe. But then we have to ask whether this does not imply a very severe diminution of the Christian hope. If Christian eschatology means no more than that the possibility of authentic existence is open to any believing individual today, then we may say that although this is much, it falls far short of that New Testament vision of a new heaven and a new earth entertained by the first Christians and presumably by our Lord himself. Pannenberg and Moltmann do much more justice to that vision and perhaps they alone are entitled to speak of Christian hope in its fullness. But they still have to show that their own talk of a resurrection of the dead is not just a relapse into mythology but can be given an intelligible and acceptable meaning in the context of our modern understanding of the universe. I would say, however, that the Moltmann–Pannenberg stress on the social and even cosmic scope of eschatology is very much preferable to the individualism of Bultmann who, in a strange way, combined elements of Lutheran pietism with his sceptical theories. Yet even in acknowledging the strength of Moltmann and Pannenberg at this point, one is bound to add that Moltmann's attempts to relate Christian eschatology to future-oriented political and social movements in the modern world are lacking in conviction, because Christian presuppositions are so different from those that govern either Marxist politics or technological planning.

We seem then to have a tied game, and cannot come down decisively on the side either of Bultmann or his opponents. Are we to say then that after nearly two thousand years of theological reflection, Christian eschatological beliefs remain as varied and even confused as they were in New Testament times? In one sense, this is true. But it is also true that during these centuries of reflection, new depths and new implications of Christian hope have been explored. The fact that it remains theologically fragmented need not worry us. If Christian hope is a total hope, then I do not think that on this side of its fulfilment we can grasp it in anything other than a fragmentary manner. In this sense we can understand Paul's cautionary words: 'Eye has not seen, nor ear heard, neither have entered into the heart of man the things which God has prepared for them that love him' (I Cor. 2, 9). The various theological interpretations of Christian hope, some individual, some social, some cosmic, some this-worldly, some other-worldly, some evolutionary, some revolutionary, some looking to the present, others to the future, are not so much rivals to each other as rather fragments of an inclusive vision that escapes us. We cannot synthesize all these theologies, but neither can we choose one of them and reject all the others. We have got to let them confront one another, correct one another, even conflict with one another, and in this dialectical procedure, both the strengths and the weaknesses of the different positions will come to light and we may hope to come closer to the total vision. To take some few steps in that direction will be our task in the concluding chapter.

Notes
[1] J. N. D. Kelly, *Early Christian Doctrines* (Fourth Edition, A. & C. Black, London, 1968), pp. 463–4.
[2] Augustine, *The City of God*, IV, 4, tr. Marcus Dods (T. & T. Clark, Edinburgh, 1871), vol. I, p. 140.
[3] Kelly, op. cit., p. 172.
[4] Irenaeus, *Against Heresies*, V, 35, tr. A. Roberts and W. H. Rambaut (T. & T. Clark, Edinburgh, 1869), vol. II, pp. 151–3.
[5] Origen, *De Principiis*, I, v, tr. F. Crombie (T. & T. Clark, Edinburgh, 1869), vol. I, p. 54.
[6] Quotations from Joachim of Fiore, *Treatise on the Four Gospels*, in Frank N. Magill, ed., *Masterpieces of Christian Literature* (Salem Press, New York, 1963), vol. I, 224–8.
[7] Rosemary R. Reuther, *The Radical Kingdom: The Western Experience of Messianic Hope* (Harper & Row, New York, 1970), p. 25.
[8] Quoted in Magill, op. cit., p. 228.
[9] Immanuel Kant, *Religion within the Limits of Reason Alone*, tr. T. M. Greene and H. H. Hudson (Harper Torchbooks, New York, 1960), p. 126.
[10] Kant, op. cit., p. 15.
[11] Albrecht Ritschl, *The Christian Doctrine of Justification and Reconciliation*, tr. H. R. Mackintosh and A. B. Macaulay (T. & T. Clark, Edinburgh, 1900), p. 284.
[12] Ritschl, op. cit., p. 433.
[13] Richard Niebuhr, *The Kingdom of God in America* (Harper Torchbooks, New York, 1959), p. 193.
[14] In my *Thinking about God* (S.C.M. Press, London, 1975), pp. 61–72.
[15] Karl Marx and Friedrich Engels, *On Religion*, ed. Reinhold Niebuhr, p. 212.
[16] Herbert Marcuse, *One Dimensional Man* (Sphere Books, London, 1968), p. 14.
[17] Reuther, op. cit., p. 141.
[18] Johannes Weiss, *Jesus' Proclamation of the Kingdom of God*, tr. R. H. Hiers and D. L. Holland (S.C.M. Press, London, 1971), p. 133.
[19] Bultmann, *Jesus Christ and Mythology* (Scribner, New York, 1958), p. 13.
[20] Weiss, op. cit., p. 135
[21] Albert Schweitzer, *The Quest of the Historical Jesus*, tr. W. Montgomery (Third Edition, A. & C. Black, London, 1954), p. 238.
[22] Op. cit., p. 397.
[23] Barth, *The Epistle to the Romans*, tr. E. C. Hoskyns (Oxford University Press, London, 1968), p. 314.
[24] Barth, *Church Dogmatics*, II/1, tr. T. H. L. Parker *et al.* (T. & T. Clark, Edinburgh, 1957), p. 634.
[25] Bultmann, 'New Testament and Mythology,' in *Kerygma and Myth*, ed. H.-W. Bartsch, tr. R. H. Fuller (S.P.C.K., London, 1957), p. 13.
[26] Bultmann, *Jesus Christ and Mythology*, p. 33.

27 Wolfhart Pannenberg, 'The Revelation of God in Jesus of Nazareth,' in *Theology as History*, ed. James M. Robinson and John B. Cobb, Jr. (Harper & Row, New York, 1967), p. 128.
28 Jürgen Moltmann, *Theology of Hope*, tr. J. W. Leitch (Harper & Row, New York, 1967), p. 165.

V

Christian Hope: A Contemporary Statement

In the remaining pages of this book, I shall set forth my own thoughts on how one might move towards a more comprehensive understanding of the Christian hope, paying attention to whatever seems worthwhile in the many theological expressions of hope that we have passed in review, and paying attention also to the modern context of philosophical and scientific ideas within which a contemporary statement has to be made if it is to carry any conviction.

My goal will be to commend a full Christian hope—a total hope. By this is understood a hope that envisions a universal renewal and restoration, yet one which also finds room for the fulfilment of each individual whom God has called into existence; a hope that would be this-worldly and evolutionary in the sense that everything that we do now in the way of building up truth, love, peace and community can be understood as co-operating with God's purposes for his creation, yet that would also be other-worldly and revolutionary in the sense that the goal would be understood as a transformed mode of existence beyond what we can visualize from our present situation; a hope that would be future in the sense that its full shape lies ahead and is not yet wholly discernible, yet also present in the sense that here and now through our communion with God and our fellowship with one another in the communion of saints we can have at least a glimpse or foretaste of eternal life. Only some such comprehensive hope, I believe, would gather up all the promises of the biblical revelation and all the insights of generations of Christian theologians. But is it all too grand and unrealistic? Is it possible to entertain such a hope with intellectual integrity in the world in which we really live—a world which, on the one hand, seems to have as many threats as promises, and, on the other, can no longer be understood in mythological ways but in terms of relativity theory, evolutionary theory and so on?

I do not think we can conscientiously hold or teach the Christian hope in anything like its traditional form as a total hope unless we are prepared to ask ourselves very seriously about its possibility in the light of all our modern knowledge about human life on this planet. When we take that knowledge into account, is the Christian hope possible? I believe that it is possible, and will try to show how this is so. But I would also want to stress that we are embarking on a very modest exercise, and so I would draw attention to the word 'possible.' I am simply trying to show the *possibility* of the Christian hope, not trying to *establish* it on general considerations. The ground of the hope is the God who has been known in Jesus Christ, and in subsequent reflection on the tradition. If we accept this hope, we accept it on the ground of Christian faith, yet we can only accept it honestly if we are persuaded that it lies within the area of what is possible.

Our discussion will fall into two parts. First, we consider the broad question of a consummation or restoration or renewal of the whole human race or even of the world, as symbolized in the tradition by such ideas as the general resurrection, the coming of the kingdom and the return of Christ in glory. In putting this broad expectation first, I think we are also recognizing that in the biblical and Christian tradition, there is concern for all mankind in its solidarity and corporate existence, rather than with individuals considered in isolation. But when we have considered this first topic, then we must go on to a second one, namely, the possibility of an eternal destiny for the individual within the broader framework.

1. *The Larger Hope*

Though it may seem strange to say so, I think it is the larger hope and the large-scale eschatology that is easier to visualize and for which analogies are more readily available. Of course, we need not and probably should not think of one final consummation beyond which no further advance or fulfilment is possible. Just as the idea of creation does not necessarily posit one particular moment of beginning, but can be seen as a continuing and perhaps even eternal process, so we may think of God as constantly bringing the creation to its consummation, and we may think of any consummation as opening the way into new possibilities of fulfilment. The process of evolution on this earth, so far as we can trace it, offers a very useful analogy. That process has gone on partly by slow and gradual developments, partly also by the attainment of critical stages when the pace suddenly quickens, a new configuration of the factors involved has come about, and something novel has emerged. I refer to such events as the emergence of the living from the non-living and then of the personal from the merely living.

If one had been able to look on the physico-chemical processes at work on earth before the emergence of living things, it would have been impossible to predict or visualize the wealth of plant and animal forms that would arise; but retrospectively the emergence of the living can be seen as the realization of a hidden potentiality of the non-living. Again, if one could have looked out on the profusion of plants and animals living on earth before the appearance of man, one could not have gained from that vista any hint of the emergence of spirit and reason and personhood, or of how the whole earth would be transformed; but again in retrospect these can be seen as potentialities contained in the matrix of matter-energy.

There is no reason to suppose that we have come to the last of such emergences, and expressions like 'the resurrection of the dead' or 'the kingdom of heaven' can be understood as pictorial or imaginative ways of pointing forward to the next emergence, the next step or stage of existence in this world. Here, I think, we are able to give an intelligible meaning in terms of modern conceptions to some of the traditional Christian symbols of hope. But one would have to add that, just as in the case of earlier emergences, the next step remains hidden so long as we are still on this side of it. This corresponds in turn to the fact that it is so difficult to specify what we mean by the Christian hope, and at this point too we may recall some of the problems that we had with the promise-fulfilment schema, and how we learned that the specification of a promise develops as events unfold themselves.

It must be noted too that in one very important respect the next threshold of emergence will be different from all those that have been crossed in the past, because for the first time it will not come about solely through the agency of natural process and natural law, but will be to some extent a consequence of human decisions and deeds. With man, the evolutionary process has become conscious of itself and has taken over a measure of responsibility for itself. We could say that along with God's creativity there is now at work man's creativity, and that the future will depend on both. It will not be simply the case that 'nature will take its course,' for more and more man influences and shapes nature; yet all power is not given into man's hands, and what he must do is help to bring about a state of affairs in which further hidden potentialities of nature (including human nature) can be released. To go back to the traditional language for a moment, we could say that man has to make ready the earth and to make ready his own heart for the advent of a new creation which God himself alone can bring. This is the co-working of God and man.

The view of consummation or renewal that I am setting out here is, of course, very close to that of several theologians of recent decades. Some of them have speculated on these matters in some detail, and it is interesting to note what they have said, and especially how they have tried to spell out their ideas (or, perhaps we should say, guesses) on the new state of affairs that might come into being on the occasion of some future emergence.

Fifty years ago, the Anglican theologian Lionel Thornton was drawing on the work of process philosophers, especially Alexander and Whitehead, to construct a dynamic theology with a definitely eschatological character. The central Christian doctrine of incarnation, he believed, ruled out both an entirely other-worldly and an entirely this-worldly interpretation of life, and so of the goal of life. He visualized a cosmic series of stages of being, each higher stage marked by an increasingly complex structure which is at the same time a higher unity. Man sums up in himself all the preceding stages and brings them into a new unity. But Jesus Christ represents still another stage. He is a 'new creation' and in him 'the human organism was taken up on to the level of deity.'[1] But Christ also introduces a new social principle into human life, and it is this that Thornton takes as his clue as he seeks to understand the consummation already being brought about through the incarnation. He finds the Pauline model of the 'body of Christ' a helpful indicator at this point. 'The individual is taken up by transformation into the organism of the new humanity. That new humanity is a new creation constituted in Christ, who is its transcending principle of unity. Within the larger whole the individual Christian is taken up by transformation to conform to its higher rhythm. His individuality is taken up in its incompleteness and carried toward actualization.'[2] Admittedly, there are some obscurities of language here. But the general picture is tolerably clear. The end is a new community in which there will be a unity that goes beyond anything we know at present, though not a devouring unity that destroys distinctions. This vision which he presented in the context of modern evolutionary thought, Thornton believed to be continuous with the patristic speculations of Irenaeus and others.

Very similar and nowadays better known is the teaching of Pierre Teilhard de Chardin. He expounds very much the same kind of evolutionary cosmos as does Thornton, though Teilhard particularly stresses the unity of the inward and the outward, the spiritual and the physical, as two aspects of a single energy. He lays great weight too on what he calls 'hominization' as a critical moment in evolution, namely the point where man begins to take over a measure of control of the world and a corresponding measure of responsibility for it. The goal of the process is designated 'omega' by Teilhard, and his under-standing of this is again in some ways reminiscent of Thornton, for it is depicted as a community which will be in some sense suprapersonal. But Teilhard's language is even more obscure than Thornton's, for we are told that this community will be 'a grouping in which person-alization of the All and personalization of the elements reach their maximum, simultaneously and without merging, under the influence of a supremely autonomous focus of union ... The goal of ourselves is not our individuality but our person; and, according to the evolutionary structure of the world, we can only find our person by uniting together.'[3] His high conception of matter and its potentialities permits Teilhard to think of the consummation as gathering up in a new unity not only persons but the whole universe. He imagines a cosmic eucharistic consecration in which the whole universe will become for us the body of Christ.[4]

In spite of his idea of hominization, I doubt if Teilhard reckons seriously with the difference which the co-operation (or non-co-operation) of man must make in the working of evolution. He tends to represent the advance toward 'omega' as an indefeasible process and underestimates human fallibility. Teilhard's theology leans toward optimism rather than hope, and I have already made it clear that hope and optimism are very different from each other. When we acknowledge that human co-operation with God is needed if the goal of a perfectly unified community is to be attained, we are admitting an element of fallibility and uncertainty into the situation. But we know that this is characteristic of hope. A genuine hope is always vulnerable, and if the vulnerability is taken away, hope has degenerated into optimism.

The recognition forced upon us in recent times that the human race may bring upon itself planetary disaster should keep us very mindful that this evolutionary way of looking toward the consummation as the next threshold of being by no means reduces it all to a natural process or an autonomous advance. Natural process has been partially displaced on earth by the more complex reality of history. On the other hand, it may be going too far to say with Leslie Dewart that 'there is no "divine plan"' and that 'history may fail' and that 'a real and eternal (more precisely, definite, irresistible) hell is a real possibility.'[5] This may, I say, be going too far, for it does not seem to reckon seriously enough with God's promise, as his utter commitment to his creation, so that he could never acquiesce in its total ruin; nor with his power to resurrect, that is to say, to bring forth the new when all avenues seem closed. But over against any easy optimism or any superficial belief that God will see everything right in the end, Dewart's words are salutary. God's kingdom cannot come until men have prepared the way for it, and therefore it cannot be something assured and guaranteed, come what may, but must remain an object of hope.

Apart from the criticism I have made of Teilhard de Chardin, I would be in agreement with both him and Thornton that the end to which we look forward in our historical epoch is a new social unity, though its nature cannot be grasped by us short of its fulfilment. This vision of the end does surely lie within the area of the possible—indeed, it fits in very well with what we know of the past development of the planet. At the same time, we can also claim that it corresponds to what Christians have expected—the resurrection of the dead, the coming of the kingdom, the return of Christ in glory, the gathering up of all things in God, or however it may have been expressed. We can say further that even if the nature of this end is in large measure veiled from us, we have an anticipation of it in Christ and in his body, which is the Christian community; and that when this end is realized, new vistas will open up beyond it. Such a cosmic vision is surely a great encouragement and source of hope to the human race as it struggles to build up peace, justice and authentic community in the world.

Any final hope for the individual can be entertained only in the context of the broader hope that has been delineated. But is there indeed any comparable hope for individuals? Or are they dispensable stepping stones to the larger hope?

2. *The Destiny of the Individual*

I do not think we can answer the questions posed at the end of the preceding section by saying that the individual must simply be sacrificed on the way to the larger goal. We may recall that the first belief in the possibility of a destiny transcending death for the individual arose out of a passionate desire for justice.[6] But what justice would there be if the goal of a fulfilled creation were at some point to be reached, but the way to that goal was strewn with the unrelieved suffering and frustration of millions of human lives? God's purpose for creation, in that case, would be just as cold and heartless as that of the revolutionary who sheds the blood of his contemporaries for the sake of a future utopia which is always in the beyond. There would be no true gathering up or summing up of all things in Christ if so much had to be discarded and if the goal demanded that people be used as means and not treated as ends.

Thus in Christian theology visions of the end have always found a place for those who have perished in the course of the historical path leading to the goal. The resurrection of the dead has meant not just the raising of human society to a new level or the attainment of a new stage in evolution, but the bringing into this new life of the faithful departed of the past.

Yet this belief in an individual destiny beyond death is one with which we have great problems nowadays. Human life seems to us to be so closely bound up with the body that we cannot envisage for it any reality when the body is dissolved. It is for this reason that I remarked that it is perhaps easier to see the possibility of a cosmic hope and to embrace it than to entertain a hope for the individual beyond death.

Am I overestimating the difficulties that stand in the way of believing that the human individual has a destiny that transcends death? Perhaps I am. In a recent article on the present state of theological thinking on these matters, Paul Badham has written: 'One of the surprising features of modern Christian thought is that there appears to be a growing tendency to repudiate or belittle any kind of belief in a future life, and yet at precisely the same time some recent writings in the philosophy of religion have shown how good a case can be made out for its possibility.'[7] The writer mentions two main approaches that have been revived and restated in recent attempts to rehabilitate the belief. One is the doctrine of an immaterial soul, associated in some way or another with the body during one's earthly life and then continuing to exist independently after the death of the body. The other is a doctrine of the resurrection of the body, though this can be worked out in ways which do not imply a literal raising and reviving of the body of flesh and blood. To these two approaches I would like to add what I think is a third possibility, though it is closer to a doctrine of resurrection than of an immortal soul—the temporal conception of selfhood as a way to establishing the possibility of a continuing existence for the individual.

Since it is this third way that I favour myself, I shall be expounding it in some detail. But first let us look at the two other possibilities.

I do not myself find the first hypothesis, the doctrine of an immaterial soul, a persuasive one. Admittedly, it has had a long history and can claim among its advocates some of the greatest philosophers of all time, such as Plato and Descartes. It still has its advocates, among them Dr. Badham to whose article we have just referred and who had earlier written a book in which he offers an able defence of the doctrine. The attraction of this view is that it seeks to do justice to the fundamental difference between body and soul and opposes every attempt to assimilate the soul to bodily process. As Dr. Badham expresses it, 'the mind or soul is a reality which is both logically and contingently distinct from the body'[8] and his argument is that only on the basis of such a distinction is it possible to formulate a valid theory of knowledge, for rational inquiry entails judgment and decision-making which it would be absurd to attribute to material entities.

With his criticism of materialism, I think we might agree. A self or soul seems to be of quite a different order from a physical body, and when we attempt to grasp it as an object of investigation, it eludes us, for it just is not objectifiable in the way that bodies are. But to try to solve the problem by moving in the direction of a Cartesian dualism (and Badham defends Descartes against some of his modern critics[9]) seems to me mistaken. The reason is that in regarding the soul as a persisting entity distinct from though somehow associated with the body, one is regarding the soul as having a mode of being analogous to that of the body. Both are regarded as 'things,' though things of very different sorts—in Descartes's terminology, a 'thinking thing' (*res cogitans*) and an 'extended thing' (*res extensa*). In trying to bring both mind and body under the category of thinghood, there is a failure on Descartes's part to take the difference radically enough.

Objections to a dualism of soul and body have multiplied in

modern philosophy, and I think that cumulatively they make the doctrine appear highly improbable. It can be criticized for an individualistic view of the self, for it seems to hold that the soul is some self-contained ready-made entity and ignores the fact that a recognizably human soul or self comes into being only through relations with other human selves (John Macmurray).[10] It can be criticized for positing an isolated subject who has then to be inserted into a world, as if the human being were not essentially and from the ground up a being-in-the-world (Martin Heidegger).[11] It can be criticized on the ground that it has not adequately considered the nature of mental concepts, which are 'verbal' rather than 'nominal' (Gilbert Ryle).[12]

Arising partly from these philosophical objections, one can state others of a more general nature. They relate to the kind of experience that a disembodied soul might have. Could this be a full human and personal existence, or could it be only a ghostly existence, like that of a shade in the underworld? There seems to be general agreement, for instance, that sense perception would not be possible, since there would be no sense organs. Dr. Badham points out that in dreams we have very vivid perceptions in the absence of any stimuli from the sense organs.[13] This is true, but surely it depends on the stimulation in some other way of the sensory areas of the brain, and it is difficult to suppose that we could have any images at all in the absence of a brain. A similar point can be made about memory. Without memory, there could scarcely be a continuing personal identity, but is memory possible without brain cells in which traces of past experiences have been stored? Most seriously of all, it is hard to see how a disembodied soul could have relations with other persons, for such relations are normally mediated by our bodies. Would a disembodied soul be like the windowless monad of Leibniz? Even if one were prepared to admit the possibility of some form of telepathy, it seems quite likely that telepathy itself depends on some as yet undiscovered form of physical energy associated with the brain.

In dealing with matters so complex and difficult, one can never be sure that all the factors have been taken into account, and those who support dualism could no doubt reply to most of these objections with further refinements of their arguments. Still, I think that the objections are formidable, and that we should look for a less vulnerable hypothesis.

So we turn to the second approach, the belief in the resurrection of the body. Incidentally, I am not able to agree with my colleague Maurice Wiles that 'there is much less difference between the two formulations in terms of a resurrection of the body and immortality of the soul than is usually claimed,'[14] for it does seem to me that a hypothesis of a resurrection of the body escapes most of the difficulties mentioned in the last paragraph. However, it brings along plenty of new difficulties of its own. Still, it is a resurrection of the body that has been the traditional Christian hope, and whatever else the expression may mean, it is clearly meant to refer to a full mode of existence beyond death, not any diminished existence as if only a part of the human person were to live on.

I need hardly say that any strictly literal belief in a resurrection of the body would be very difficult to hold. It is hardly conceivable that all the particles that once constituted the body of a person now deceased could be reassembled, and in any case the particles constituting anyone's body are themselves constantly being replaced throughout life. Furthermore, if precisely the same kind of body of flesh and blood were to be reconstituted, would it not be subject to the same physiological and biochemical laws that governed it in earthly life, so that it would in due course disintegrate once more? It may be true that in the history of the Christian Church most Christians have believed in this crudely literal idea of resurrection, but we have seen that in the New Testament itself Paul distinguished a spiritual body from the physical body and believed that it is the spiritual body that is raised.[15] Sophisticated theologians have followed him in maintaining that the resurrection body would be different from the body of flesh and blood, even if they have supposed the two to be continuous in some way. Origen, for instance, says: 'Neither we nor the divine scriptures maintain that those long dead will rise up from the earth and live in the same bodies without undergoing any change for the better.'[16] Contemporary theologians who teach the resurrection of the body, such as Pannenberg, are likewise clear that they do not mean simply the revivification of the body of flesh and blood, though I did complain that one of the weaknesses of their position is that their affirmative teaching remains unclear.[17]

But is talk about a 'spiritual body' just a blurring of the issue? I do not think so. A body is not just a framework of flesh and blood. It can also be considered philosophically as our means of insertion (or presence) in a world of things or persons or, for that matter, angels or spirits or whatever other beings there may be. It was some such ontological understanding of the term 'body' that the writers of the report, *Doctrine in the Church of England*, must have had in mind when they wrote of the resurrection body as an 'appropriate organ of expression and activity.'[18] If such a body were to be the bearer of memory, which would seem to be essential for the maintaining of personal identity, then it would surely need to stand in some relation to the body of flesh and blood, especially to the brain. Could we suppose that there might be some pattern or structure of energy which survives the destruction of the body which is ours in this life, and that this is made up of that single energy that has both mental and physical characteristics, and that there would be possible for it a sufficient measure of 'expression and activity' as would permit the kind of operations and relationships which, as we have seen, would be very difficult to conceive if we thought in terms of a 'naked' immortal soul? This resurrection body, which would have at least some formal continuity with the old physical body, would be what has sometimes been called a 'transformation body.'

If one is to take seriously the findings of psychical research—I confess I am very sceptical myself, though I would not be so arrogant as to dismiss these findings out of hand—then it might be claimed that there is plenty of evidence for the existence of such transformation or transformed bodies, existing in a different state from the bodies we know in our everyday lives. The resurrection appearances reported in the New Testament (or, at least, some of them) could also belong here.

When matter was conceived in the old-fashioned way as made up of solid bits of inert stuff, then the idea of a transformed resurrection body may have seemed only a wild imagining, and the idea of a spiritual body even a contradiction in terms. But now that matter is itself understood as a form of energy, and now that with every year the nature of matter-energy is found to be more and more complex and mysterious, one cannot rule out the possibility of some refined or rarefied type of body, different from the body of flesh and blood but sufficiently continuous with it to carry on its experiences beyond death. Admittedly, the appeal here may seem to be to the gaps in our knowledge. But is this all that can be said? Will the gaps ever be filled in a way that will exclude the possibility? Physicist Harold K. Schilling suggests that with every new discovery, new reaches of the unknown are exposed at the same time. In particular, with every discovery about the nature of matter-energy, we discern more of 'the limitless internal depth and content of physical reality.'[19]

The possibility of a resurrection of the body in some form or other is certainly one that cannot be dismissed. On the other hand, when attempts are made to speculate on the nature of the resurrection body, the hypotheses become so ingenious and far-fetched that they strain credibility to the utmost. One thinks, for example, of John Hick's suggestion that there might be 'the divine creation in another space of an exact psycho-physical "replica" of the deceased person.'[20] This may well have been shown by Hick to lie within the bounds of possibility, but it is such a remote and even bizarre possibility that it is hard to see that it offers much support to belief in a life to come. Perhaps in the present inconclusive state of debate about a resurrection of the body, there is nothing to do but wait for the moment that John Hick has elsewhere called 'eschatological verification.'[21]

I have indicated that it is to a third approach to the problem that I am myself attracted. This third view is built on a consideration of the temporality of the self. That is to say, we try to see the self as a pattern in time, just as a body is a pattern disposed in space. I would like to mention here an enigmatic but highly suggestive expression used by Samuel Alexander, when he spoke of 'time as the mind of space,' and explained this by saying that 'time as a whole and in its parts bears to space as a whole and its corresponding parts a relation analogous to the relation of mind to its equivalent bodily or mental basis.'[22] Though I accept that the soul is inseparable from the body (and so the view I am expounding is closer to the resurrection than the immortality hypothesis), soul and body are distinct in the sense that soul is to be understood in terms of time, body in terms of space. Of course, the unity is the psycho-physical being of man, which is also spatio-temporal. Incidentally, in saying that the soul is inseparable from the body, I am not for a moment saying that it is a mere epiphenomenon of the body. On the contrary, the soul is the way by which a human person comes to terms with time so as to rise above mere transience and even to have a taste of 'eternal life,' as was claimed in the first chapter of this book.[23] I would be quite happy to follow the Aristotelian and Thomistic fashion of calling the soul the 'form' of the body, but such a form is itself active and creative.

If we suppose then that it is characteristic of a human self to transcend the mere succession of instants and to hold together past, present and future in a 'span of time,' so that even in the midst of time he has a hint of eternity, may we then apply this analogy to the experience of God? We, in a fragmentary manner, gather up tiny segments of past and future through memory and anticipation. May we suppose that God gathers up all time, so that past and future are both present in their fullness to him? 'For a thousand years in thy sight are but as yesterday when it is past, and as a watch in the night' (Ps. 90, 4). In this sense, the past that has perished for us is still present in God, gathered up in the simultaneity of his universal experience.

We can link this with the claim made in the last section that the kingdom of God or the resurrection of the dead can be understood as the next critical emergence in evolution, and here we may recall Thornton's point that each stage sums up or recapitulates all the preceding ones—man sums up and brings into a new personal unity the merely physico-chemical and biological stages that have gone before, and Christians claim that Jesus Christ sums up in himself humanity in a still higher unity that is coming to be—the body of Christ. Could we suppose then that our destiny as individuals is not to live on as immortal souls or to be provided with new bodies, but to be summed up or gathered up in the experience of God as the people we are or have been in our several segments of time and in our bodies?

Again, I think one can provide analogies for the concentration of a duration of time into a moment when the successive instants are experienced simultaneously. When you see a play or read a novel, the plot unfolds itself and the characters develop; but when you get to the end, it is all present in its fullness and the mind can grasp all the connections and relationships that have been brought to light. Picasso's 'Guernica' is a picture which sets aside all the normal conventions of space and time, before and after, up and down and simply throws at us, as it were, persons, things, animals, actions from a city that was bombed in the Spanish civil war; and we find that these fragments in their simultaneity reveal the terror and tragedy of the situation. A devout Catholic, kneeling in prayer before the Blessed Sacrament after the mass, contemplates in its ineffable fullness the mystery that was presented step by step in the successive moments of the eucharist. Very interesting too are the many reports that have been preserved of how people very near to death—drowning people, for instance—have the experience of seeming to relive their whole lives. Raymond Moody has collected reports of the experiences of a great many people who had either been pronounced clinically dead or had a very close brush with death, but had subsequently revived. A panoramic review of life is a regular item in these reports. 'This review,' Moody says, 'can only be described in terms of memory, since that is the closest familiar phenomenon to it, but it has characteristics which set it apart from any normal type of remembering. First of all, it is extraordinarily rapid. The memories, when they are described in temporal terms, are said to follow one another swiftly, in chronological order. Others recall no awareness of temporal order at all. The remembrance was instantaneous; everything appeared at once, and they were able to take it all in with one mental glance. However it is expressed, all seem in agreement that the experience was over in an instant of earthly time.'[24]

These experiences, I suggest, can afford some clue of what it would mean for the past to be renewed and summed up in the experience of God, as he brings his creation and his own striving in the creation to a new consummation.

Dr. Badham, in the article to which I have already referred, wonders whether I am simply saying that God will remember us, and he rightly points out that just to be remembered would be much less than what has been understood by eternal life, in which surely the person concerned would on his side have new experiences, including a deeper awareness of and communion with God.[25] But although I have used the analogy of memory, I have avoided speaking of the memory of God, for when I say that the past is still present to God, I have in mind a much more lively and realistic relation than simply memory. I do not mean that we shall remain fixed and unchanged for ever in God's memory, like a fly caught centuries ago in amber or a mammoth trapped and preserved intact in a glacier. I mean something much more dynamic, namely, being taken up and participating in the life of God himself. Here I might recall what was said in an earlier chapter about the resurrection of Jesus Christ,[26] and I would see him as the first fruits of the general resurrection.

Dr. Badham remarks that 'the vivid picture of a future life' which I set forth is not securely derived from the temporal analogy from which I set out. This picture is in terms of the purgation of souls and their growth in a commonwealth of love, in which they have deepening communion with God and with each other. Now, if it were only a static past which God preserved, then any talk of growth would be impossible. But I believe that God is in fact healing the past. In an earlier writing I expressed this by saying: 'No individual existence that has been called out of nothing will utterly return to nothing, but will move nearer to the fulfilment of its potentialities, as the horizons of time and history continually expand and it is set in an ever widening reconciling context.'[27] What I mean is that it is no dead or frozen past that is present to God but a past which is itself being transformed as God brings about his consummation.

Am I talking nonsense, as if one could somehow change the past? No, I am prepared to accept with St. Thomas that even 'God cannot make what is past not to have been.'[28] Incidentally, I am also allowing to death its finality, as the cut-off point of a finite human existence. But what cannot be changed about the past is its factuality, its happenedness, so to say. What has been and what has been done remain. However, though one cannot change the facts of the past, the value of these facts can be changed and often is changed. It is in this sense that one can quite properly say that the past can be healed and transformed. The hardship that someone suffered at a certain period of her life seemed like a bitter evil, but it has turned out to be the adversity coefficient that has made that person a woman of character. What twenty years ago I thought was a smart piece of business now fills me with regret and repentance. What I experienced as a bitter disappointment, I now recognize to have been very much for my good. The person whom I used to despise I now see in quite a different light and desire a new relation with him. These transformations of the past take place as we move into new and broader contexts and are able to see new connections and relationships and effects.

But now we again extend these experiences by analogy to God. Can we believe that God is gradually healing and transforming the past, so that it can find its place in that future consummation which we call the kingdom of God or the resurrection of the dead or the return of Christ or whatever mythological expression is preferred? God is not changing the past by changing the facts that have happened (this is not possible even for him) but by bringing it into what I have called 'an ever wider reconciling context.' The supreme example of this is the cross of Christ which is turned from evil to good and finds its completion in the resurrection—and we remind ourselves that Easter is not a reversal of Good Friday but its conversion. This is God's reconciling work, and it reaches into all time, including the past which is still present to God. It is the costly atoning work of God, by which he draws out and absorbs and overcomes the poisons of history.

There is a mythological representation of this retroactive work of
God in the story of Christ's descent into hell. To be sure, the biblical
foundations for this story are flimsy and obscure. I shall mention only
one passage: 'For Christ also died for sins once for all, the righteous
for the unrighteous, that he might bring us to God, being put to
death in the flesh but made alive in the spirit; in which he went and
preached to the spirits in prison, who formerly did not obey when
God's patience waited in the days of Noah ... For this is why the
gospel was preached even to the dead, that though judged in the
flesh like men, they might live in the spirit like God' (I Pet. 3, 18–20
and 4, 6). The words are capable of several interpretations but have
usually been taken to mean that in the interval between the crucifixion and the resurrection Christ went to Hades, the place of the
departed, and liberated the souls in prison through the preaching
of the gospel. The descent into hell came to be incorporated into the
Apostles' Creed as an article of faith, and the imagery was elaborated
in medieval art. That imagery is perhaps most familiar to English-
speaking Christians through Archbishop Maclagan's hymn for Holy
Saturday, of which I quote some verses:

> In the gloomy realms of darkness
>   Shines a light unknown before,
> For the Lord of dead and living
>   Enters at the open door.

> See! he comes a willing Victim
>   Unresisting hither led;
> Passing from the cross of sorrow
>   To the mansions of the dead.

> Lo! the heavenly light around him
>   As he draws his people near;
> All amazed, they stand rejoicing
>   At the gracious words they hear.

> Patriarch and priest and prophet
>   Gather round him as he stands,
> In adoring faith and gladness
>   Hearing of the piercèd hands.

Oh, the bliss to which he calls them,
Ransomed by his precious blood,
From the gloomy realms of darkness
To the paradise of God.[29]

This is, of course, pure mythology, but like much other mythology, it does seek to express a truth. This is the truth I have been trying to express in a more abstract language, the truth that God's atoning work can be retroactive and that even the 'spirits in prison' can be brought out of their dead frozen past to share in renewal and resurrection.

One might also mention the strange practice in the very early days of Christianity whereby some people were baptized on behalf of the dead. 'What do people mean by being baptized on behalf of the dead? If the dead are not raised, why are people baptized on their behalf?' (I Cor. 15, 29). We usually pass discreetly over these words of Paul, assuming that they refer to some absurd superstition which no one could take seriously. But whatever the practice may have been supposed to mean, it seems to imply that Christ's saving work is no more restricted in time than it is in space, and this is a point that should be taken seriously.

Up till now I have been building the case for what I have called a 'third approach' to the question of life beyond death on the basis of our understanding of time as we experience it in human life. It is important that we should have this basis in experience, which allows us to give some recognizable content to such ideas as the transcending of mere transience and even of eternal life here and now. It has also enabled us to make some speculations about time in God's experience, on the analogy of our own. But I think that the whole position can be strengthened and receive independent confirmation if we now take into account the understanding of time that has emerged in modern science, especially in relativity theory. The interesting point is, of course, that the concept of an absolute present or universal 'now' has been put radically in question, and therefore so have the concepts of an absolute past and an absolute future.

In the traditional way of conceiving them (and I suppose it is still the commonsense way that we employ in daily life), space and time were taken to constitute an absolute independent frame of reference, within which everything takes place at precisely definable times and places. Space was conceived like a huge container—one is almost tempted to say, like a huge box, except that it had no sides or lid or bottom to it, for space was also considered to be infinite in extent. Time, on the other hand, was like a flux, carrying everything along at a uniform rate from the 'not yet' of the future through the fleeting 'now' of the present into the 'no longer' of the past. The scheme presupposed an absolute 'now,' extending through the whole of space and dividing the past from the future. Every event could be located on one side or the other of the dividing 'now,' except, of course, the events going on right now, that is to say, in the simultaneity of this present moment throughout infinite space. In some sense, too, it was believed that what is now has alone full reality—the past has ceased to be and the future has not yet come into being. The real, or, at any rate, the actual, consists of that thin slice of existence that extends infinitely through space at this precise moment. See Figure 1.

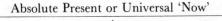

Absolute Future

Absolute Present or Universal 'Now'

Absolute Past

Figure 1

The first upset to this traditional understanding of space and time came in the seventeenth century when the Danish astronomer Ole Rømer demonstrated that light travels at a finite speed. It follows that when we look up into the sky at night, we are not only looking into space but into the past. Some of the light now impinging on our sight may have been on its way for a very long time indeed, so that we are looking back through many centuries, though the star is present to our vision now. Again, although the whole sky and all the objects in it are simultaneously present to our senses, we are in fact looking over a wide range of times. We see the moon as it was a little over a second ago, Sirius as it was more than eight years ago, and the more distant the object in space, the more remote it is in the past. Perhaps indeed it has ceased to exist, though it is still present to our senses. A German poet, impressed with the new understanding of the universe that was opening up, wrote:

Vielleicht vor tausend Jahren schon
Zu Asche stob der Stern!
(Perhaps a thousand years ago
The star crumbled to ash.)

Admittedly, Rømer's discovery that we perceive objects in the past still did not upset the idea of an absolute present or universal 'now,' for by fairly simple calculations one could compensate for the effects on our perception arising from the time that light takes to travel, and so arrive at an objective view of what is taking place at any moment. One would then have to distinguish between the perceived now and the objective now. This has some importance for our own problem of eternal life and the continuing presence of the past to God, for it shows us that even in our own experience the past may be present to us not merely in memory but in direct perception, so we can have some idea of what it means to say that the past is present to God.

However, it was only with Albert Einstein's relativity theory that the concept of absolute simultaneity or a universal now really broke down. He illustrates what he calls the 'relativity of simultaneity' by a fairly simple case. Let us suppose that a train is travelling along an embankment. Two flashes of lightning take place, one at the point A at the rear of the train and the other at point B at the front. To an observer standing on the embankment at point M, midway between A and B, the flashes would appear simultaneous. But to a second observer on the train who happened to be passing point M just as the first observer saw the flashes, the flash at B would be seen earlier than the flash at A, because he is moving toward the beam of light coming from B and away from the other. Presumably if a second train were passing in the opposite direction, an observer on it would see the light from A before the light from B. 'We arrive at the important result: Events which are simultaneous with respect to the embankment are not simultaneous with respect to the train and *vice versa* (relativity of simultaneity). Every reference body (co-ordinate) system has its own particular time; unless we are told the reference body to which the statement of time refers, there is no meaning in a statement of the time of an event.'[30] See Figure 2.

To understand the implications of this for our concept of time, it will be helpful to attend to some remarks of Sir Arthur Eddington, which in turn will lead us to redraw in a quite different manner the diagram (Figure 1) in which we represented the traditional or

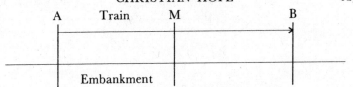

Figure 2

commonsense view of time. 'Father Time,' wrote Sir Arthur, 'has been pictured as an old man with a scythe and an hour-glass. We no longer permit him to mow instants through the world with his scythe; but we leave him his hour-glass.'[31] An hour-glass consists of two cones, one of which we can take as representing the absolute future, the other the absolute past, while the narrow neck at which they join is the here and now of a particular observer. The wedge shaped ever broadening region between the two cones has taken the place of that infinitely thin absolute 'now' which separated past and future in Figure 1, and this wedge shaped area is not absolutely past or future but a neutral zone. Of course, here on earth the neutral zone, like the time difference between Einstein's two observers, is so small as to be negligible for all practical purposes, but as we take in larger regions of the universe, it increases. To return to Eddington for a moment: 'Suppose that you are in love with a lady on Neptune and that she returns the sentiment. It will be some consolation for the melancholy separation if you can say to yourself at some—possibly prearranged—moment, "She is thinking of me now." Unfortunately a difficulty has arisen, because we have had to abolish "now." There is no absolute "now" but only the various relative "nows," differing according to the reckoning of various observers and covering the whole neutral wedge which, at the distance of Neptune, is about eight hours thick. She will have to think of you for eight hours on end in order to circumvent the ambiguity of "now." '[32] See Figure 3.

What is the significance of these scientific notions of time and space (or space-time) for the views I was putting forward about the past being still present to God and alive in God, and about his power to heal and transform even the past? I think the significance is quite considerable, and should make it clear that to talk of God in such ways is not to indulge in a kind of theological science-fiction. I think there are three points of importance. 1. We have seen that even on the level of finite experience it is possible for the past and even the

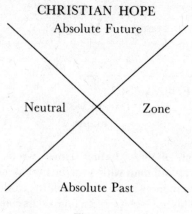

Figure 3

distant past to be present not just in memory but in direct perception; and further, we have seen that the absolute or universal 'now' has been abolished, and with it the rigid separation of past and future. So we have analogies in our own experience for some of the temporal enigmas or paradoxes that we introduced, and this assures us that they are not nonsensical. 2. When we try to extend the analogy to God, it is important to remember the difference as well as the similarity. Relativity theory does not by any means subvert the difference between past and future—these remain, as we see in Figure 3, even if there is a large region outside of them. But if we are thinking of God, then what does vanish in Figure 3 is the point of intersection of the two cones, the here and now that characterizes any finite experience. We can say either that God occupies every point in space-time or we can say that he is 'outside' of the space time continuum, and perhaps we have even to say both if he is both immanent and transcendent. What we cannot say is that he is at some particular here-now and nowhere else—that is excluded by the logic of God-talk, for it could be said only of a particular being, and God is simply Being itself. This means that the very obvious restrictions which apply to our own capacity for perceiving the past or for circumventing the 'now' are removed in the case of God, who must have a freedom from time and for time beyond our imagining. 3. Finally, the abandonment of the conception of absolute space as what I called a 'container' is also significant, for that conception led to many dualisms and separations—the dualisms of time and space, of mind and matter, even of God and the world, and it is these dualisms in turn that have made any idea of life beyond death seem improbable. Perhaps at this point we get a new light on that saying of S. Alexander, quoted earlier, that time is the mind of space. Thomas F. Torrance has pointed out in his writings that the old container view of space (he prefers to call it the 'receptacle' view) almost inevitably led in the direction of materialism and atheism. The newer view (which he calls the 'relational' view) has reunited space and time and seen space-time not as a pre-existing container but as the ordering of an organic universe. 'This has had the effect of shattering the receptacle idea and of undermining the radical dualism to which it had given rise in modern philosophy and theology as well as science.'[33]

In this section I have been expounding what I have called a 'third approach' to the problem of individual destiny as an alternative to the traditional theories of the immortality of the soul or the resurrection of the body. I think it is sufficiently distinct to be called a third view, though I also believe that it includes what is important in a doctrine of resurrection. My reasons for preferring it have now become clear. They may be summed up as follows: this view coheres quite readily with a 'larger hope,' as expounded in the preceding section, and it is the larger hope that is more important; this view is well founded in our experience of time, and this in turn, we may hope, provides an anaology for the divine experience; the view also accords with the understanding of time in modern physical science, and even gets confirmation from it; finally, I think that this view involves us in fewer bizarre speculations than some of its rivals.

But as a Christian theologian, I would have to add that my hope that human beings have an eternal destiny does not rest on ingenious theories about a life 'after' death or 'beyond' death. We remind ourselves that we have simply been trying to show that such hopes are possible and cannot be dismissed as nonsense or lacking any rational defence. If Heidegger's understanding of human existence or Einstein's theories about space-time or any other resources of philosophical or scientific thought help toward this, then the theologian is entitled to make use of such resources. But his belief rests finally on this, that if God is indeed the God of love revealed in Jesus Christ, then death will not wipe out his care for the persons he has created.

Notes
[1] L. S. Thornton, *The Incarnate Lord* (Longmans Green, London, 1928), p. 245.
[2] Thornton, op. cit., pp. 291–2.
[3] P. Teilhard de Chardin, *The Phenomenon of Man*, tr. Bernard Wall (Collins, London, 1959), pp. 262–3.
[4] P. Teilhard de Chardin, *Hymn of the Universe*, tr. Gerald Vann (Collins, Fontana Library, London, 1970), p. 27.
[5] Leslie Dewart, *The Future of Belief* (Herder & Herder, New York, 1966), p. 196.
[6] See above, p. 40.
[7] Paul Badham, 'Recent Thinking on Christian Beliefs: The Future Life,' in *The Expository Times*, vol. LXXXVIII (April, 1977), p. 197.
[8] Paul Badham, *Christian Beliefs about Life After Death* (Macmillan, London, 1976), p. 133.
[9] Badham, op. cit., pp. 97–100.
[10] John Macmurray, *The Self as Agent* (Faber & Faber, London, 1957).
[11] Martin Heidegger, *Being and Time*, tr. J. Macquarrie and E. S. Robinson (S.C.M. Press, London, 1962).
[12] Gilbert Ryle, *The Concept of Mind* (Hutchinson, London, 1949).
[13] Badham, op. cit., p. 134.
[14] Maurice Wiles, *The Remaking of Christian Doctrine* (S.C.M. Press, London, 1974), p. 146.
[15] See above, p. 79.
[16] Origen, *Contra Celsum*, tr. H. Chadwick (Cambridge University Press, 1965), V, 23, p. 281.
[17] See above, p. 77.
[18] *Doctrine in the Church of England* (S.P.C.K., London, 1936), p. 209.
[19] Harold K. Schilling, *The New Consciousness in Science and Religion* (United Church Press, Philadelphia, 1973), p. 118.
[20] John Hick, *Death and Eternal Life* (Collins, London, 1976), p. 279.
[21] John Hick, *Philosophy of Religion* (Prentice-Hall, Englewood Cliffs, 1963), pp. 101–2.
[22] Samuel Alexander, *Space, Time and Deity* (Macmillan, London, 1920), vol. II, p. 38.
[23] See above, p. 23.
[24] Raymond A. Moody, *Life after Life* (Bantam Books, New York, 1976), p. 64.
[25] Badham, loc. cit., p. 198. I do not know how seriously I should take Dr. Badham's further point that all things recalled and brought to their fulfilment in God 'would logically include parasites, harmful bacteria and long extinct animals.' Presumably the same objection could be made to all from Paul to Teilhard who have visualized all things gathered up in God. The answer might be that since there is surely play as well as utility in the abundance of the creation, the long extinct animals might well add to the beauty and variety of the consummation. God, I think, would be on the side of the conservationists! Parasites and the like raise the question of natural evil. They may be degenerate forms of life which are untransformable and can only be left embedded in the past. On the other hand, if it is not too fanciful to imagine a renewed heaven and earth as well as a renewed society, it might be said that parasitism is not so far removed from symbiosis, and might be transformed into it. But I do not think it necessary to venture into such speculative questions.
[26] See above, pp. 79–80.
[27] John Macquarrie, *Principles of Christian Theology* (Revised Edition, S.C.M. Press, London, 1977), p. 361.
[28] Thomas Aquinas, *Summa contra Gentiles*, II, 25.
[29] W. D. Maclagan, *Hymns Ancient and Modern*, No. 122. There is a slightly different version in *The English Hymnal*, No. 120.

[30] Albert Einstein, *Relativity: A Popular Exposition* (Eighth Edition, Methuen, London, 1924), p. 26.
[31] A. S. Eddington, *The Nature of the Physical World* (Cambridge University Press, 1929), p. 48.
[32] Eddington, op. cit., p. 49.
[33] T. F. Torrance, *Space, Time and Incarnation* (Oxford University Press, 1969), p. 58.

Index of Names